T0167752

Distributed Power in the United States

This report was co-written by authors from the Hoover Institution and the Brookings Institution.

HOOVER INSTITUTION

SHULTZ-STEPHENSON TASK FORCE ON
Energy Policy

B | Energy Security Initiative
at BROOKINGS

Jeremy Carl
Research Fellow,
The Hoover Institution
Director of Research,
Shultz-Stephenson Task Force
on Energy Policy

David Fedor
Research Analyst,
Shultz-Stephenson Task Force
on Energy Policy,
The Hoover Institution

Pedram Mokrian
Principal, Mayfield Fund
Contributor, Shultz-Stephenson
Task Force on Energy Policy,
The Hoover Institution

Jelena Simjanović
Senior Research Assistant,
Shultz-Stephenson Task Force
on Energy Policy,
The Hoover Institution

David Slayton
Commander, United States Navy
National Security Affairs Fellow,
The Hoover Institution

Amy Guy Wagner
Senior Consultant, Energy and
Environmental Economics, E3

John Banks
Nonresident Fellow,
Energy Security Initiative,
The Brookings Institution

Kevin Massy
Assistant Director,
Energy Security Initiative,
The Brookings Institution

Lisa Wood
Executive Director,
IEE Nonresident Fellow,
Energy Security Initiative,
The Brookings Institution

Distributed Power in the United States

Prospects and Policies

Edited by Jeremy Carl

Foreword by
George P. Shultz and Strobe Talbott

HOOVER INSTITUTION PRESS
STANFORD UNIVERSITY STANFORD, CALIFORNIA

www.hoover.org

Hoover Institution Press Publication No. 632

Hoover Institution at Leland Stanford Junior University,
Stanford, California 94305-6010

First printing 2013
19 18 17 16 15 14 13   7 6 5 4 3 2 1

Manufactured in the United States of America

The paper used in this publication meets the minimum Requirements of the American National Standard for Information Sciences—Permanence of Paper for Printed Library Materials, ANSI/NISO Z39.48-1992. ∞

Cataloging-in-Publication Data is available from the Library of Congress.
ISBN: 978-0-8179-1584-1 (cloth. : alk. paper)
ISBN: 978-0-8179-1586-5 (e-book)

CONTENTS

ABBREVIATIONS

ACEEE	American Council for an Energy-Efficient Economy
AEIC	American Energy Innovation Council
AMI	Advanced Metering Infrastructure
ARPA-E	Advanced Research Projects Agency—Energy
ARRA	American Recovery and Reinvestment Act 2009
CAES	Compressed Air Energy Storage
CAISO	California Independent System Operator
CCA	Community Choice Aggregator
CEDA	Clean Energy Development Authority
CES	Clean Energy Standard
CESA	Clean Energy States Alliance
CHP	Combined Heat and Power
CIGRE	International Council on Large Electricity Systems
CLEER	Clean Local Energy Efficiency and Renewables Act
CPUC	California Public Utility Commission
CSI	California Solar Initiative
DER	Distributed Energy Resources
DG	Distributed Generation

DoD	Department of Defense
DOE	Department of Energy
DPS	Distributed Power Systems
DR	Demand Response
DSCR	Debt Service Coverage Ratio
DSIRE	Database of State Incentives for Renewables & Efficiency
EE	Energy Efficiency
EERS	Energy Efficiency Resource Standard
EID	Energy Improvement District
EISA	Energy Independence and Security Act 2007
EPA	Environmental Protection Agency
EPAct	Energy Policy Act 2005
EPRI	Electric Power Research Institute
ESA	Electricity Storage Association
FERC	Federal Energy Regulatory Commission
FIT	Feed-In Tariff
FOB	Forward Operating Base
GHG	Greenhouse Gas
IC	Internal Combustion
IEE	Institute for Electric Efficiency
IOU	Investor Owned Utility
IREC	Interstate Renewable Energy Council
ITC	Investment Tax Credit
LCOE	Levelized Cost of Electricity
LOLP	Lost of Load Probability
MACRS	Modified Accelerated Cost-Recovery System
MADRI	Mid-Atlantic Demand Resource Initiative
MLP	Master Limited Partnership
NARUC	National Association of Regulatory Utility Commissioners

NEM	Net Energy Metering
NERC	North American Electric Reliability Council
NIST	National Institute for Science and Technology
NNEC	Network for New Energy Choices
NREL	National Renewable Energy Laboratory
NYISO	New York Independent System Operator
OATT	Open Access Transmission Tariff
ORC	Organic Rankine Cycle
PHEV	Plug in Hybrid Electric Vehicle
PPA	Power Purchase Agreement
PRD	Price Responsive Demand
PURPA	Public Utility Regulatory Policies Act of 1978
PTC	Production Tax Credit
PUC	Public Utility Commission
PV	Photovoltaic
QF	Qualifying Facility
RAM	Reverse Auction Market
RAP	Regulatory Assistance Project
REC	Renewable Energy Credit
REPPS	Rucksack Enhanced Portable Power System
RPS	Renewable Portfolio Standard
SAIDI	System Average Interruption Duration Index
SAIFI	System Average Interruption Frequency Index
SCADA	Supervisory Control and Data Acquisition
SGIP	Self-Generation Incentive Program (California)
T&D	Transmission and Distribution
UPS	Uninterruptible Power Supplies
V2G	Vehicle-to-Grid
VNM	Virtual Net Metering
WACC	Weighted Average Cost of Capital

LIST OF FIGURES
AND TABLES

TABLES

FOREWORD

Many energy analysts have noted the potential for DPS to become a major part of our electricity infrastructure. The recent drop in key technology costs has brought this potential closer to reality. But in this rapidly developing field, the great progress on the technological front has yet to be fully matched by progress in policymaking. And major questions of affordability, integration, and security remain to be answered before we can determine what role distributed energy sources should play in our future energy system.

DPS offers the potential for more reliable, secure, and green energy. It can encompass everything from fuel cells providing electricity and clean water to a remote army outpost in Afghanistan to solar panels on the roof of a home in Arizona. At the same time, possible pitfalls related to DPS use must be seriously and realistically addressed before we make a major commitment to a distributed energy future.

This report provides a comprehensive survey of the current technology and policy landscape of DPS and offers recommendations for its future use. As it highlights the importance of an emerging, critical policy issue that has not received the full attention it merits until now, we believe the report will be useful to policymakers and practitioners alike.

> George P. Shultz
> *Thomas W. and Susan B. Ford*
> *Distinguished Fellow*
> *The Hoover Institution*

———————

The provision of reliable and secure energy to meet the growing demands of this century, in a way which mitigates the adverse effects of climate change, is an existential challenge to the human enterprise. A failure to meet the challenge would pose grave risks to the functioning of world economies, the nature of societies, and our endangered ecosphere. In fact, the degree of success in this area will be a big determinant of whether this will be the best or the worst century for humankind.

One proposed method for improving the economic, environmental, and energy-security performance of the U.S. power sector is the adoption of distributed power systems (DPS), a combination of distributed generation and electricity storage technologies. In this inter-disciplinary paper, scholars from the Brookings Institution's Energy Security Initiative and the Hoover Institution's Energy Task Force evaluate the case for greater deployment of DPS. The chapters which follow set out a number of considered conclusions and clear recommendations for all policymakers who have a responsibility for ensuring the security and sustainability of our energy system now and for future generations.

> Strobe Talbott
> *President*
> *Brookings Institution*

EXECUTIVE SUMMARY

The U.S. power system is the backbone of the country's economy. Yet, with growing stress on the aging existing electricity grid, increasing integration of information technology with the power sector infrastructure, and an imperative to reduce the environmental impact of power generation, the system faces an unprecedented range of economic, environmental, and security-related challenges. The situation has given rise to increased interest in the potential for Distributed Power Systems (DPS): a combination of distributed sources of power production, and distributed energy storage. This study examines the economic, environmental, and energy security case for DPS. It finds that increased penetration of DPS has the potential to make a significant positive contribution to the U.S. power system. It also finds a strong case for DPS as a resource for the defensive and offensive operations of the U.S. military.

In general, the economics of DPS are still unproven: using a traditional cost-comparison model, our analysis shows that most DPS technologies are currently uncompetitive when compared with central station fossil fuel generation. However, in certain regions of the country, some DPS technologies are already cost competitive with large-scale fossil fuel generation. These include IC engines and gas turbines with combined heat and power, and medium and community-scale wind generation. The economic analysis also shows that a moderate price on carbon of $30 would increase the competitiveness of some renewable energy DPS applications. Moreover, many DPS technologies, such as solar photovoltaic, are realizing rapid declines in unit costs that are likely to continue with sustained research, development, and deployment of such systems. Economic analysis and extensive outreach to power sector stakeholders show that the benefits of DPS are location and time-specific, and that DPS are more valuable in areas with high levels of system congestion or peak demand and no excess capacity.

There is also widespread agreement among power sector stakeholders that existing economic models do not capture the full range of potential benefits that DPS can provide. These include improved efficiency of the distribution system, reduced strain on the grid during peak-demand period, greater reliability, environmental and land-use benefits, possible job creation, the harnessing of untapped energy resources, and other region-specific benefits. They also include the security value of DPS, both as a means of decreasing the vulnerability of the civilian grid to disruption and attack and as a resource for the defensive and offensive operations of the U.S. military. In addition, many stakeholders see that there is insufficient information on the full spectrum of costs and benefits of DPS.

Federal and state policymakers have an opportunity to better capture the economic, environmental, and energy security benefits of DPS through the implementation of policies that correct market failures, provide incentives, remove barriers, and promote the exchange of information and education.

To realize the full potential of DPS, the federal government should: set broad energy policies that account for the externalities of carbon dioxide and other emissions; promote sustained technology research and development; conduct research on the impact of DPS penetration on both reliability and security; support DPS-related knowledge sharing and awareness; and use procurement both in the civilian and military sectors to increase DPS competitiveness through increased scale.

The U.S. military has a particularly compelling incentive to adopt DPS, which can help it meet its renewable energy and energy efficiency goals; improve the security of power delivery to bases at home and abroad; and provide advantages for expeditionary activities in theater. The military should consider distributed generation and microgrids as an essential part of its electricity generation strategy, and should develop and deploy DPS technologies that increase the efficiency of personnel in theater.

State governments should take a lead in DPS-specific policy-making. They should use policy tools that differentiate among DPS systems according to size. For small-scale customer generation, state regulators and energy planners should encourage net metering, reduce technical and non-technical barriers to interconnection, and implement pricing mechanisms that accurately value the power produced from DPS. For larger systems that sell power into wholesale markets, state policymakers should adopt limited financial incentives aimed at increasing the competitiveness of DPS over time. Stakeholders agree that storage and combined heat and power (CHP) have particular potential for improving the efficiency and economics of the U.S. power sector and, therefore, should be priorities for targeted policy support.

The increased penetration of DPS has the potential to make a significant positive contribution to the U.S. power system and to the energy needs of the U.S. military. As policymakers strive to meet the challenges of the power sector in the 21st century in an economic and environmentally responsible way, this paper provides them with a set of options for realizing that potential.

ACKNOWLEDGMENTS

The authors would like to thank a number of people involved in the research, writing and production of this study. First, they would like to thank Charles Ebinger, the director of the Brookings Energy Security Initiative, and George Shultz, chair of the Shultz-Stephenson Task Force on Energy Policy at the Hoover Institution, who conceived of the project. Ebinger provided insights to the conclusions and recommendations, and was a keen reviewer of many iterations of the report. Secretary Shultz offered key strategic direction, cogent critiques of early drafts, an invaluable perspective, and insights from his extensive experience in policymaking at the highest levels. Ambassador Thomas Stephenson has supported the work of the Shultz-Stephenson Task Force on Energy Policy with both his generosity and his counsel. The authors would also like to thank Yinuo Geng and Caldwell Bailey for their significant substantive contributions and Govinda Avasarala for his input and coordination efforts. Brandon Smith served as intern on this project and was helpful with research assistance. The authors owe a special thanks to Richard Kauffman, Nathan Hultman, Snuller Price,

Bradley Schoener, and Ted Piccone for their timely reviews and feedback. The authors are also grateful to the academics, government and industry officials, and regulators for responding to various survey requests and for being so forthcoming with their experience and insights. Gail Chalef, Robin Johnson, and Chris Krupinski at Brookings along with Jennifer Presley, Barbara Arellano, and Jennifer Navarrette and the rest of the Hoover Institution Press team were invaluable in the editing and production process.

INTRODUCTION

The U.S. power sector faces the biggest overhaul in its history. Designed for the supplies and demands of the twentieth century, the current electric grid requires substantial investment to continue to provide reliable power for a growing, electricity-dependent population. The pressures on the power system are compounded by two major trends that will have a profound impact on the provision and consumption of electricity: the integration of large amounts of renewable energy generation capacity and the advent of the "smart grid."

Concerns over carbon emissions and climate change have led to federal- and state-level efforts to reduce the environmental mpact of electricity generation. Spurred by an array of incentives and mandates, and facilitated by falling costs of technology, the United States has deployed a vast quantity of large-scale renewable-energy installations over the past decade.[1] Such power sources provide significant reliability challenges as grid operators and utilities attempt to both integrate output from intermittent generation sources and reduce reliance on fossil fuel-based power while keeping the lights on. Much of the added renewable energy generation capacity is located in—or planned for—areas a long way from demand centers. The extra infrastructure required to transmit and distribute the output from these new generation sources presents an enormous financial, logistical, and legal challenge.

This challenge of renewable integration comes at a time when the existing power grid is facing unprecedented demands. While electricity remains the backbone of economic activity, enthusiasm among policymakers and end-users for a more flexible and efficient power system is leading to the integration of digital technology into the physical electricity infrastructure and the creation of a "smart grid." However the full realization of the smart grid concept will require resolution of a host of issues including new pricing structures, cost-allocation, and consumer acceptance. According to security analysts, the integration of information technology into the power system will also make the electricity supply more vulnerable to network-wide cyber-attacks or infiltration by domestic or foreign actors.[2]

The situation has given rise to a growing interest in the potential for Distributed Power Systems (DPS), a combination of distributed generation sources (also called distributed generation) and distributed grid storage. DPS technologies include rooftop solar installations, "microwind" turbines, electrochemical fuel cell systems, and fossil fuel-based combined heat and power (CHP) applications. They also incorporate distributed energy storage systems, including advanced batteries and vehicle-to-grid (V2G) systems.

The broad range of technologies and applications that can be categorized as DPS means that any assessment of their collective costs, benefits, and potential—and the appropriate level of policy support for them—must proceed cautiously.

Advocates of DPS see them as a means of harnessing local sources of generation to enable commercial, residential, and industrial electricity consumers to bypass the centralized system of generation and dispatch and, in many cases, to meet their own electricity needs. They see DPS as having the potential to stabilize and support the grid by relieving congestion while deferring or avoiding the construction of new centralized power plants by offsetting end-user demand.

Advocates also highlight the ability of many distributed technologies to increase the efficiency of power delivery through avoided transmission and distribution (T&D) losses, reduced capital expenditures on T&D, the conversion of waste heat and energy to useful power, and the ability to harness distributed renewable resources through systems such as rooftop solar installations. Others stress their potential to decrease electricity-system vulnerability through the diversification of the power supply portfolio and the "islanding" of generation and distribution. They also see the potential for DPS technologies to be adopted by the military to improve the operating efficiency of bases and expeditionary missions. The most ardent supporters of DPS see them as holding the potential to revolutionize the U.S. power sector through the replacement of the existing power system with new local markets for electricity based on networks of small-scale generation and informed consumption.

Critics of DPS highlight the high cost of distributed sources of power generation relative to centralized power stations and the danger of subsidies and incentives for DPS technologies creating unsustainable industries. They also point out the negative disruptive effects of attempting to integrate small-scale generation and storage systems into a power infrastructure not designed to accommodate them. In a sector that depends more than any other on predictability and reliability of operations, they argue, any attempt to move away from a highly centralized and controlled system to a new paradigm based on the aggregation of numerous independently run assets comes with enormous direct and indirect costs.

This paper aims to address the role and potential for DPS by addressing four basic questions:

- What are the current economic, environmental, and energy security costs and benefits of increased penetration of DPS relative to the centralized model of power generation?
- What policies and regulations are currently in place to promote DPS and how effective are they?
- What are the potential benefits of increased penetration of DPS and what are the barriers to achieving them?
- What, if anything, can and should federal and state governments do to further encourage DPS?

The report is divided into four sections:

- Chapter 1 places the evaluation of DPS in a historical context, provides a definition and overview of each of the DPS technologies, and provides a summary of notable DPS programs and initiatives to date.
- Chapters 2 and 3 assess the economic, environmental, and security-related costs and benefits of DPS relative to centralized power generation. The economic and environmental analyses rely on a quantitative model developed by Energy and Enviromental Economics, E3, an independent energy economics consultancy. Chapter 3 provides an overview of the security-related benefits of DPS drawing on existing literature.
- Chapters 4 and 5 address the policy landscape for DPS, with the former addressing the range of existing and proposed policies that have a bearing on DPS adoption at

both the federal and state levels. Chapter 5 reports on the results of the primary policy-related research conducted for this study. The research team canvassed a wide spectrum of stakeholders in the U.S. power system to establish respondents' views on the current role and potential benefits of DPS, the effectiveness of current policies and incentives related to DPS, the barriers to DPS, and the desirability and effectiveness of a range of proposed mechanisms to improve the performance and penetration of DPS.

- Based on the findings of the preceding sections, Chapter 6 outlines the report's findings and conclusions and proposes a set of recommendations for policymakers looking at DPS as a potential tool to meet state and federal energy policy goals.

Expert Forum

"We've got to get back to that era when we said, 'Here's a problem. What can we do about this problem?' And then solve problems. Then we'll begin to get somewhere."

—George P. Shultz, *Thomas W. and Susan B. Ford Distinguished Fellow, The Hoover Institution*

In October 2011, the Energy Security Initiative at Brookings and the Hoover Institution's Shultz-Stephenson Task Force on Energy Policy hosted experts in Washington, DC, to discuss opportunities and challenges around the development of distributed power systems in the United States. Throughout their dialogue, these practitioners from federal and state government, civil society, business, and defense drew from their personal experiences to shed light on key DPS dynamics. These comments serve as a useful adjunct to, and commentary on, the overall conclusions reached in our study. We have shared their words following each chapter of this study, as a way of showing how several panels of experts reacted to and amplified the work we had undertaken.

Conference participants included:

Sharon Burke
Assistant Secretary of Defense for Operational Energy Plans and Programs, U.S. Department of Defense

Tom Casten
Chairman, Recycled Energy Development

Ken Colburn
Senior Associate, Regulatory
Assistance Project

Steve Corneli
Senior Vice President,
Sustainability, Policy, and
Strategy, NRG Energy

Vice Admiral Philip Cullom
Director, Energy and
Environmental Readiness
Division, U.S. Navy

Charles K. Ebinger
Director, Energy
Security Initiative

Kevin Fox
Interstate Renewable
Energy Council

Peter Fox-Penner
Principal, The Brattle Group

Allen Friefeld
Executive Vice President,
External Affairs,
Viridity Energy

Andrew Karsner
Executive Chairman,
Manifest Energy

Hank Kenchington
Deputy Assistant Secretary,
Research and Development,
Office of Electricity Delivery
and Energy Reliability,
U.S. Department of Energy

Dennis McGinn (Vice
Admiral, Retired)
President, American Council
on Renewable Energy

Pedram Mokrian
Principal, Mayfield Fund

Rick Morgan
Commissioner, District of
Columbia Public Service
Commission

James Rogers
Chairman, President,
and Chief Executive Officer,
Duke Energy

Bradley Schoener
Energy Portfolio Manager,
The MITRE Corporation

George P. Shultz
Thomas W. and Susan B. Ford
Distinguished Fellow,
The Hoover Institution

Peter W. Singer
Director, 21st Century
Defense Initiative

Strobe Talbott
President, The Brookings
Institution

Amy Guy Wagner
Senior Consultant, Energy and
Environmental Economics, E3

Robert Weisenmiller
Chairman, California Energy
Commission

> "*I've been working on this [energy] issue in one way or another for forty years now. In the last few years, I feel for the first time as though we're really beginning to get somewhere, because there really is a recognition that it's a genuine big-time problem. The present situation is not satisfactory and you see things beginning to change. People's attitudes changing; new things coming into play. If we can just keep at it in the kind of spirit exhibited today, we're going to get there from here.*"
>
> —George P. Shultz, *Thomas W. and Susan B. Ford*
> *Distinguished Fellow, The Hoover Institution*

OVERVIEW OF DISTRIBUTED POWER SYSTEMS

1.1 DPS in Context

For the past century, the U.S. electric power system has operated predominately on a model of centralized electricity generation, with power being delivered to end-users via a long-distance transmission and distribution infrastructure. The original rationale for the centralized model was economically compelling. Economies of scale in the construction of generation assets coupled with the highly capital-intensive nature of generation and transmission construction led to the emergence of local monopolies in the form of franchises responsible for discrete geographic service. The requirements to balance loads and ensure reliability of supply led to the development of an interconnected system. By the 1950s, the vast majority of U.S. power demand was served by the electric utility industry with the exception of a small number of industries that continued to rely on self generation. Driven by inexpensive fuels and unlimited capacity growth, electricity generation grew by an average of 6.5 percent per year from 1950 to 1960 and by an average of 7.5 per year from 1960 to 1970, creating a robust demand for the output of the central station power system.[1] As the system grew, the laws and regulations designed to protect the consumer from the natural monopolies helped to expand the centralized grid model.

The Move to Decentralized Generation

The trends in operating efficiency, cost, and size that supported a centralized power system have leveled out over the past forty years. Beginning in the 1970s, the electric utility industry changed from one characterized by decreasing marginal costs to one of increasing costs.[2] The energy crises and oil price shocks at the beginning and end of the 1970s, stricter air quality regulations, rising interest rates, and escalating costs of nuclear power led to increased costs of building large-scale power plants, while a drop-off in the rates of electricity demand growth made the case for new additions of such plants less attractive. At the same time, the market for non-utility generation also began to open up. The National Energy Act of 1978, which encompassed the Public Utility Regulatory Policies Act (PURPA) was enacted to address a nationwide energy crisis. PURPA heralded a new era of distributed generators by enabling small power producers to sell generation from "qualifying facilities," or QFs, to utilities without discrimination. Qualifying facilities were accorded the right to sell energy or capacity to a utility; the right to purchase certain services, such as back-up power, maintenance power, and interruptible power from utilities; and relief from certain regulatory burdens.

Under the terms of PURPA, utilities subject to federal regulation were required to purchase electricity from QFs at "avoided cost," the cost the utility would have to pay to generate the electricity itself. While the Federal Energy Regulatory Commission

(FERC) created a set of rules for the implementation of PURPA, the interpretation and implementation of PURPA—and particularly the "avoided cost" calculation—was left to the discretion of the states and their public utility and public services commissions.[3] The consequence of this state-level implementation was a patchwork of varying policies for the integration of QFs into the power generation mix. Generous "avoided cost" levels led to the policy proving so popular in California that the state suspended its PURPA system in 1985 due to surplus supply from operators of QFs. PURPA implementation, together with associated tax incentives, contributed to the addition of 12,000 MW of geothermal, small-scale hydro, solar, wind, and biopower generation facilities through the 1980s in the United States, more than half of which were in California.[4] In most other states, however, PURPA was not enacted with such enthusiasm and FERC acknowledged the uneven nature of the policy's implementation.[5] California's interpretation of PURPA provided the basis for many current "feed-in tariff " policies, through which utilities offer fixed-price, fixed-term contracts for power generated from specified sources.

While the early 1980s saw a spike in the number of small-scale power producers, the requirement for small generators to sell their power at a state-determined "avoided cost," combined with falling natural gas prices, made many of the long-term QF contracts uneconomic relative to centralized generation.[6]

Several other legislative and regulatory developments in the following decade continued to support distributed generation. The Energy Policy Act of 1992 began the process of opening access to interstate transmission lines to independent power producers, thereby creating a competitive wholesale electricity market. The move to deregulate (or restructure) *retail* electricity markets in the late 1990s gave an even larger boost to distributed generation. By 2000, fifteen states had enacted restructuring legislation that challenged the dominance of large utilities by enabling smaller power producers to compete for retail customers.

In the past decade, several factors have combined to hinder the development of centralized power generation while increasing the attractiveness of distributed generation. According to IHS CERA, the cost of constructing new power plants increased 131 percent between 2000 and 2008,[7] owing in large part to rising raw material and labor costs, a shortage of skilled and specialized engineers, and a global increase in demand for similar equipment and services. New large-scale generation has also faced several non-financial obstacles. New coal facilities are threatened both by new environmental regulations on greenhouse gas (GHG) emissions and potential increased generation costs if carbon is priced. Pending EPA regulations for sulfur dioxide (SO_2), nitrogen oxide (NO) and mercury (Hg) may shut down substantial portions of coal-fired power in the United States while causing many remaining coal power assets to require costly retrofits. Water usage rules also threaten to impede the build-out of large-scale generation plants, evidenced by the federal ban on "once-through" cooling, which has had a negative effect on new power plant construction. Even for cleaner-burning natural gas, regulations and rules on emissions have created considerable uncertainty. A potential rebirth of new large nuclear facilities in the United States, already in doubt owing to financial and regulatory concerns, has been thrown further into question amid public safety concerns after the Fukushima disaster in Japan.

Large scale renewable generators also are facing severe challenges of land use and transmission capacity. Generators located in remote regions where renewable resources are abundant—such as wind resources in the plains of Wyoming, Montana, and the Dakotas and solar in the Mojave Desert—will require the construction of significant amounts of new transmission infrastructure to reach load centers. According to the Electric Power Group's report for the California Energy Commission,[8] it takes eight to ten years to permit, construct, and build a new high voltage transmission corridor. Environmental considerations are also an issue for such projects: large solar projects in the desert have faced strong opposition to their land use and impact on endangered species, while proposed wind farms have faced local opposition on environmental and aesthetic grounds.

At the same time that large-scale generation has faced an increasing number of challenges, advances in technology have increased the competitiveness of small-scale generation by further driving down the cost of modular power-generation and storage systems and enhancing the options for communications between small generators, utilities, and end-users. New grid technologies including real-time metering, communication, and storage devices have increased the potential for networking energy sources at a community level.

Federal and state-level efforts to incentivize and mandate the build out of lower-carbon power generation capacity have added to the economic attractiveness of many DPS applications through loans, grants, tax incentives, portfolio standards, and other mechanisms. Interest from the private sector, which is more likely to consider investments in DPS than in large generation owing to lower capital costs and greater innovation potential, has also helped make DPS more attractive. Finally, new markets mechanisms also are being considered that will enable distributed generators to compete with larger incumbent sources of generation. Grid operators such as PJM, New York Independent System Operator (NYISO) and California Independent System Operator (CAISO) are considering changes to allow distributed loads and storage resources to provide ancillary services competing with natural gas generators.

1.2 Definitions

Distributed power systems (DPS) are a combination of distributed sources of generation (often termed "DG") and distributed storage. They are also referred to as distributed energy resources (DER), dispersed generation, embedded generation, and on-site generation.[9] There is far more existing literature on the definition of distributed generation than on distributed storage. The definition of distributed generation is informed by three principal considerations: the nature of the generator's output, its location, and its size. There is substantial variation in the definition of DG as illustrated by examples from the following organizations:

- **Institute of Electrical and Electronics Engineers:** "the generation of electricity by facilities that are sufficiently smaller than central generating plants so as to allow interconnection at nearly any point in a power system."[10]
- **North American Electric Reliability Corporation:** "a generator that is located close to the particular load that it is intended to serve. General, but nonexclusive, characteristics of these generators include: an operating strategy that supports the served load, and interconnection to a distribution or sub-transmission system (138 kV or less)."[11]
- **United States Congress:** "an electric power generation facility that is designed to serve retail electric consumers at or near the facility site."[12]

- **International Council on Large Electricity Systems (CIGRE):** "not centrally planned, today not centrally dispatched, usually connected to the distribution network, smaller than 50–100 MW."[13]

For the purposes of this study, DPS are defined as:

Selected electric generation systems at distribution level voltages or lower whether on the utility side of the meter or on the customer side; and distribution-level electricity storage applications.

This definition is explained below according to its constituent parts.

"Selected electric generation systems . . . and distribution-level electricity storage applications": This study focuses on an exclusive subset of technologies that constitute the most significant components of DPS applications. As with the general definition of DG, the technologies that qualify for consideration are diverse. Ackermann et al provide an excellent overview of the electricity-generating technologies that can be considered as DG (see Figure 1.1).

For the purposes of this study, the definition of DPS technologies has been reduced to a set of eight applications that constitute, in the view of the research team, the principal elements of distributed generation and storage. These applications are a combination of renewable and fossil fuel generation sources.

Solar: Systems that use either solar photovoltaic technology to convert sunlight directly into electricity or solar thermal technology to concentrate solar heat to drive a turbine for electricity production.

Wind: Systems that use wind-driven turbines to create electricity.

Combustion Engines: Reciprocating engines, spark-ignited, or compression-ignited piston-driven engines that run on natural gas or liquid fuels and generate electricity.

Microturbines: Combustion turbines that convert fuel (usually high-temperature, high-pressure gas) into mechanical output,

FIGURE 1.1 TECHNOLOGIES FOR DISTRIBUTED POWER

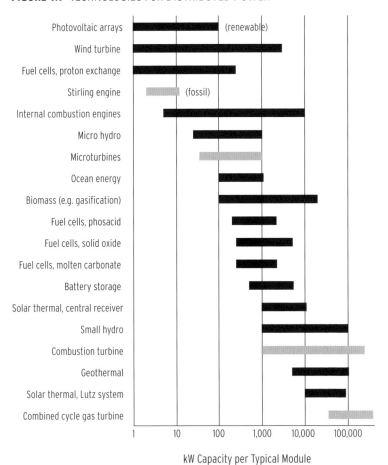

kW Capacity per Typical Module

Source: Technologies and capacity data from Ackermann et al, 2001

which is then converted into electricity. Most commonly comprise a compressor, a combustor, a turbine, an alternator, a recuperator, and a generator.

Combined Heat and Power (CHP): Applications, located near the point of consumption, that simultaneously produce useful thermal heat and harness process heat for the production of electricity. (It should be noted that CHP is not included in Ackerman's description, as it is an application rather than a specific technology—see section 1.3 for more details).

Micro Hydropower: Applications that use flowing water to create mechanical energy, which is then converted to electricity.

Fuel Cells: Electrochemical devices that convert a fuel source (such as methane or hydrogen) into electricity.

Storage: Both electrochemical devices that convert electricity into chemical energy and then reverse the process for the provision of power (i.e. batteries); and devices that convert electricity to potential mechanical energy (compressed air, pumped water), to be reconverted to electricity when required. (See section 1.3 for more detail on DPS technologies).

". . . at distribution level voltages or lower": One of the most challenging definitional tasks in discussing distributed generation is the scale of applications. As the definitions above show, some organizations prefer to address the scale question in terms of nameplate capacity while others prefer to address the issue from the perspective of the point at which applications connect to the grid. This study adopts the latter definition, focusing on applications that are situated close to load.[14]

1.3 Overview of DPS Technology

Distributed generation—the process of generating electricity at small scale in the vicinity of the load center—is an established concept and one with a long history. Even after the advent of alternating current transmission lines and increases in turbine efficiency that made large, centralized power generation possible, electricity consumers found numerous uses for distributed generation. Industrial customers have long relied on on-site generation to harness more economic sources of power than those available from the grid, while facilities with critical power needs such as hospitals and military installations have relied on on-site generation for back-up generation.[15] As stated above, this study focuses on eight distinct DPS technologies, which are explained here in greater detail.

Solar

Solar energy is the most abundant form of energy in the world: the solar energy striking the Earth's surface in one hour is equivalent to the total global energy consumption for all human activities in one year.[16] The United States has some of the world's highest solar energy potential. The solar industry has recently made substantial breakthroughs on cost, with some solar panels now below the $1/peak watt.

The United States is poised to continue to be a global leader in solar installations in the coming years and has shown historically strong growth by more than doubling its new installed capacity from 2009 to 2010. With 956 megawatts (MW) of new solar system installations in 2010, the U.S. solar market ranked fourth globally.[17] The $6B U.S. industry employs an estimated 100,000 according to the Solar Energy Industries Association.[18] The major challenge that the industry faces is that of scale. By the end of 2010, the United States had 2,593 MW of installed solar capacity;[19] to place this figure in perspective, it is equivalent to one-third of the capacity of the Grand Coulee Dam (7,079 MW peak).

FIGURE 1.2 FALLING ROOFTOP SOLAR PV COSTS IN CALIFORNIA

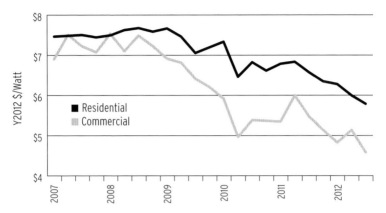

Source: GoSolarCalifornia public database
[Average real quarterly completed costs, not including subsidies, for host customer-owned rooftop PV systems under the California Solar Initiative, nameplate]

In addition to ever decreasing costs and increasing efficiencies of the actual solar panels, new improvements in balance-of-system costs such as inverters, power electronics, and wiring alongside financing and installation will continue to drive up the performance while at the same time reducing cost of distributed solar energy.

Wind

Wind power has become the most widely adopted renewable generation resource in the United States, accounting for 26 percent of all new electric generating capacity in 2010. The industry grew by 15 percent in 2010 to 5,116 MW of new wind installations, bringing total capacity in the United States to over 40 GW.[20] Between 2000 and 2010, wind generation capacity increased at an average annual rate of 150 percent.[21] The cost of wind power has continued to drop such that wind power on an installed capacity basis is often competitive with conventional generation technologies. However, the output of wind turbines is dependent on local atmospheric conditions and cannot be dispatched like fuel-driven generation technologies. This creates high variability in power output onto the grid and in turn poses operational challenges for transmission and distribution systems.

FIGURE 1.3 DISTRIBUTION OF THE PURCHASERS OF U.S. WIND POWER (CATEGORIZED BY THE OFF-TAKE AGREEMENTS)[22]

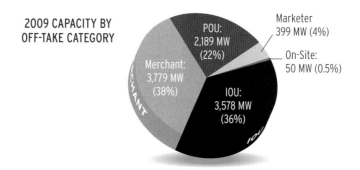

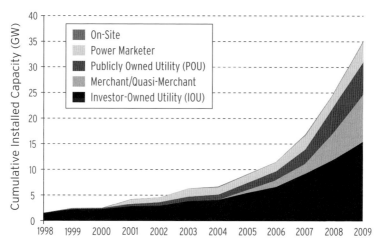

Source: Berkeley Lab estimates based on AWEA project database

The primary innovations in the industry have been around the improvements in blade design, the development of turbines that can capture wind at higher elevations, and the development of turbines and systems capable of operating offshore. Several new designs have been suggested for wind turbines in order to harvest more wind power at lower costs, including various high altitude wind technologies and new designs using jet-engine architectures.[23]

Market penetration of smaller scale wind turbines, which include all technologies that are less than 100 kW per unit, remains low, accounting for 100 MW of total installed capacity in the United States as of 2010.[24] This is due to a number of factors, including intermittency of power generation, noise consideration, availability of land, and lack of financing options. Lower unit costs ($/kW) and extraction of greater power per acre of land have been the primary factors driving up the maximum capacity of turbines over the past twenty years, with some individual turbine ratings now exceeding 3 MW. There has been a recent trend in wind farm development toward small clusters of large turbines to feed power to rural communities. Such projects rely on the dual use of land areas with farming as the primary economic activity, and wind turbines added as an additional source of revenue.

Combustion Engines

The most common form of distributed generation technology historically has been the reciprocating internal combustion (IC) engine. With over 9,000 MW of installed capacity in the United States, the IC engine accounts for almost 75 percent of all fossil fuel-driven distributed generation units.[25] Diesel and natural gas are the most common fuels used in such engines with the former used in compression ignition engines, and the latter in spark ignition engines. Other spark ignition fuels include biogas, landfill gas, and propane. IC generators are often referred to as "generator sets" or "gensets" because they are a combination of an IC engine, a generator, and various ancillary devices that together form a distributed power generation unit. IC generators typically range in capacity from a few kilowatts to 5 MW and can be installed in a modular fashion to meet varying size and load needs. The advantages of this technology lie in its low relative cost, high reliability, long operating life, short startup times, and the high availability of fuel sources. The IC engine also has high part-load efficiency, meaning that it can match or follow the electric load demand within a 30–100 percent load range both cost effectively and with little decrease in efficiency.

The major disadvantages of IC engines are their relatively high emissions (in particular, nitrous oxide, NOx) and low efficiencies, typically in the 25–33 percent range. To meet emissions requirements, most IC engine power generators use expensive post-combustion emission control systems, or are operated on an emergency only basis for a limited number of hours per year. As a result, such generation technologies are often not considered a viable option for energy applications, and are typically omitted from any energy-only comparisons with other distributed generation technologies.

The global market for generators, estimated at $11.5B in 2010,[26] is dominated by a set of applications including standby and emergency back-up power, for example in remote cell-tower back-up in the telecom industry and for back-up power and portable power needs in the construction industry. This market has been dominated historically by the diesel engine. However, recent adoption of stringent air quality regulations globally has shifted demand to other gas-based engines, bringing the global share of annual demand for generators to 69 percent in 2010.[27] The installed capacity of distributed resources in emergency/standby applications accounts for 79 percent of the total capacity, while providing merely 2 percent of the total power produced.[28]

FIGURE 1.4 INSTALLED CAPACITY OF DPS BY APPLICATION (MW) AND SHARE OF POWER GENERATED BY DPS APPLICATION (MWH)

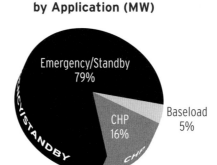

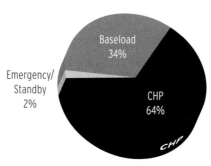

Source: As reported in "Backup Generators (BUGS): The Next Smart Grid Peak Resource," National Energy Technology Laboratory, April 2010, with data from "The Installed Base of US Distributed Generation," 2005, Resource Dynamics Corporation, Vienna, VA, data for 2003.

Microturbines

Microturbines are electricity generators that burn gaseous and liquid fuels in a turbine to create high-speed rotation that drives an electrical generator, typically ranging between 30 to 250 kW. Microturbines can operate on two principles: (i) Brayton cycle and (ii) Rankine cycle. The most popular form of microturbine technology operates on the principle of the Brayton cycle, where air is compressed, heated, and expanded to produce power. This is the same thermodynamic cycle as that in centralized turbine power plants, only on a much reduced scale. Microturbines are able to run on a variety of fuels, including natural gas, sour gases (those with high sulfur content), and liquid fuels such as gasoline, kerosene, diesel, and LPG.

The electrical conversion efficiency of microturbines using the Brayton cycle ranges from 20–35 percent. This is often higher than the combustion engine counterpart but not high enough to provide sufficient economic returns on a power generation basis, and is typically used where the thermal output of the turbine can be used locally (as in combined heat and power: see the following for details). Microturbines are also used in resource recovery applications where byproduct and waste gases that would otherwise be flared or released into the atmosphere from landfills or coal mines are used to generate power.

Microturbines that use the same thermodynamic principle as the steam engine are based on a process known as the Rankine cycle. In these systems, a working fluid, typically water, is boiled in an evaporator into a vapor phase that expands to drive a turbine/generator. A turbine technology known as the Organic Rankine Cycle (ORC) that uses an organic, low boiling point working fluid in place of water is used where lower temperature heat sources are available, such as in waste heat

FIGURE 1.5 OUTPUT AND EFFICIENCY OF VARIOUS MICROTURBINE MODELS

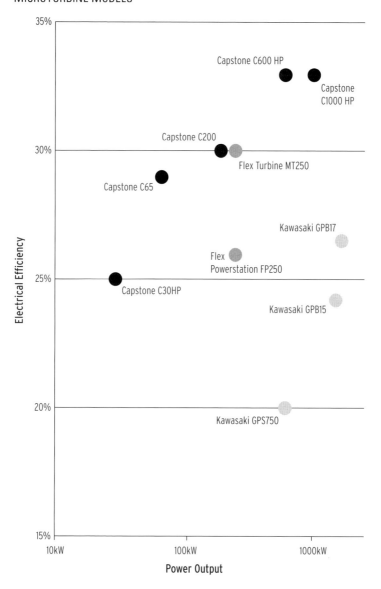

Source: Product data compiled from manufacturer websites, 2012

recovery systems. Since low embedded thermal energy or low quality fuel resources that would have otherwise been wasted are used in such microturbine applications, conversion efficiencies range between 10–20 percent. Low grade waste heat can be found in many industrial processes and exhausts from internal combustion engines, while low quality fuel resources can be found in landfills, agricultural wastes, and other industrial byproducts.

Combined Heat and Power (CHP)

Combined Heat and Power (CHP) does not represent a specific technology but an integrated energy system that provides the simultaneous production of both electricity and heat from a single fuel source. CHP accounts for nearly 8 percent of the power generated in the United States and represents the largest deployment of distributed generation technologies.[29] These combined benefits save U.S. building and industry operators an estimated $5B annually.[30]

The untapped potential for CHP is vast: according to Oak Ridge National Laboratory, CHP could save the United States 5.3 quadrillion British Thermal Units (Btu) of energy by 2030—equivalent to half of the energy consumed by U.S. households—and could reduce carbon dioxide emissions by 800 million metric tons per year.[31]

CHP systems are typically found in one of two configurations: power generation (turbine or engine) with waste exhaust heat recovered and reused locally, and heat or steam generation with a steam turbine used to generate power as a byproduct of heat or steam generation.

In the first configuration, the high thermal output of exhaust gases from engines or small turbines (which can range from

800° F to 1100° F) can be used directly for many applications, including production of steam or hot water, absorption cooling, space heating, and a diverse set of industrial applications (which account for 43 percent of global demand for heat).[32]

In the second configuration, the thermal energy from an existing operation is recycled through the production of steam for the production of power. Applications include coke ovens, glass furnaces, silicon production, refineries, pipeline compressors, petrochemical processes and the burning of flared gas from blast furnaces, refineries, or chemical processes.

Micro and Small Hydropower

Hydropower is the dominant source of renewable power generation in the world, accounting for 16 percent of the world's total electricity supply and 87 percent of global renewable energy supply.[33] The majority of this power, in excess of 90 percent, is generated from very large, gigawatt-scale power plants, which are massive environmental, financial, and technical undertakings.

Small, distributed hydropower generation applications can take advantage of the availability of available sites along rivers and canals; they have a relatively light environmental footprint, are flexible in power output, can be used as energy storage, and are a reliable baseload generation resource. "Low-head" hydropower, based on a low-head dam where the water drop is less than 65 feet, is emerging as a new alternative to high-head dams. "Run-of-the-river" systems harness moving water to produce energy without the need for large storage reservoirs.

Small hydro facilities may prove a viable option to take advantage of the vast underdeveloped hydro resources in the United States which represent upwards of 30,000 MW of new, untapped capacity.[34] Moreover, uprating or re-commissioning

FIGURE 1.6 MEDIUM, SMALL, AND MINI/MICRO HYDROPOWER CAPACITY IN THE U.S.

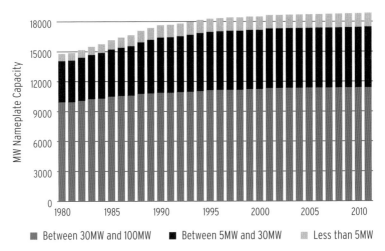

■ Between 30MW and 100MW   ■ Between 5MW and 30MW   ▦ Less than 5MW

Source: chart by authors with data from EIA Form 860 (2011); nameplate installed capacity for currently operating plants

of existing facilities may also prove to be a feasible means by which to increase the installed hydropower base since an estimated 97 percent of 79,000 dams in the United States are currently not generating any power.[35]

Fuel Cells

Fuel cells are electrochemical devices that convert chemical energy from a fuel source to generate electricity by means of a chemical oxidation/reduction reaction. The principle of the fuel cell was developed in the 1830s; however the first commercially viable applications were not available until over a century later for NASA's Project Gemini in the early 1960s. Fuel cells hold tremendous promise as a power generation technology due to their fuel flexibility, their ability to scale across applications from stationary power generation to transportation to mobile applications such as laptop computers, their theoretically high efficiencies, and their simplicity in operation since they have no moving parts. As a result, the fuel cell industry has continued to garner interest from both government research interest and private capital alike.

The end markets for fuel cell technologies include uninterruptible power supplies (UPS), combined heat and power (CHP), auxiliary power units, and portal power for military and remote monitoring applications. Early interest in these markets has resulted in a 10-fold increase in the fuel cell stacks sold from 2007 to 2010, bringing the global number of stacks shipped to 140,000, and over $750 million in revenues in 2010.[36] Approximately half of fuel cell shipments in 2010 were stationary power generation fuel cells, with the United States remaining one of the top four markets, in addition to Germany, Japan, and South Korea.

Storage

Energy storage technologies enable an offset in time between power generation and power consumption. This ability to store energy has a profound impact not only on the physical characteristics of the power grid, but also on the financial and investment strategies of power market participants. Inexpensive storage therefore has the potential to revolutionize the way that electricity grids are operated and dispatched. Although the impacts of storage and the large market need are well understood, very few storage installations are in actual operation in the United States. These are primarily limited to large-scale pumped hydro installations and a limited number of grid-scale batteries. The viability and economic feasibility of grid-integrated systems remains a topic of great interest, garnering hundreds of millions of dollars of public and private capital for investments in R&D and demonstration facilities.

There are a variety of potential energy storage technologies either currently available or under development, each having a unique set of operational, performance, durability, capacity, and cycling characteristics. There are also a host of applications for energy storage each with their own operational, physical, and cost requirements. Although the advancement of storage technologies is likely to have a profound impact on the transportation sector (through use in electric vehicles) and consumer electronic applications, the scope of this discussion is limited to larger scale, power system deployments.

Storage technology costs and application values in power systems are typically classified by their discharge capacity (MW) and energy storage capacity (MWh), which define the amount of energy that can be stored and how quickly that power can be provided on demand. Using this classification, we can define the four broad categories of energy storage technologies based on their applications, which are as follows:

Power Quality and Uninterruptible Power Supplies (UPS): These applications require ultra-fast response with short duration. Response time required is typically on the order of seconds or less, but discharge is limited to very short durations not exceeding several minutes. Flywheels and super capacitors, which have short response times and limited storage capacity, are suitable for UPS applications.

Fast Response: These are generally configured to deliver fast response and medium duration power output of between one and four hours. Fast response storage technologies include lithium ion and lead acid batteries. A subset of this category is

FIGURE 1.7 DISCHARGE TIME AT RATED POWER AND SYSTEM POWER RATING OF VARIOUS ENERGY STORAGE TECHNOLOGIES

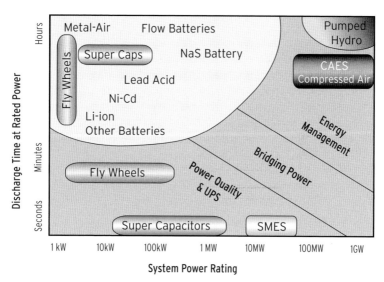

Source: Mokrian, P., Modeling and assessment of electricity market initiatives, PhD Dissertation, Stanford University, 2009.

"networked storage" such as V2G applications that use plug-in electric vehicles as a grid storage mechanism.

Bridging Power Applications: These applications, which include transmission and distribution support and temporary load shifting, require medium response times typically on the order of several minutes but have energy storage capacity of several hours. Flow battery technologies, sodium sulfur (NaS) batteries, and next generation small-scale compressed air energy storage (CAES) can respond relatively quickly, but take some time to switch from charging to discharging modes.

Bulk Energy Management: These applications include large-scale CAES and pumped hydropower storage, have low response

Similar to battery technologies, a fuel cell stack comprises an electrolyte sandwiched between a negative anode and a positive cathode. The primary difference between fuel cells and batteries lies in the fuel cell's ability to continuously produce power so long as there is a supply of fuel and oxygen present. Hydrogen is continuously fed at the anode while oxygen is supplied at the cathode. Given that pure hydrogen is not currently an abundant fuel source, high temperature fuel cells such as molten carbonate and solid oxide fuel cells can internally reform light hydrocarbon fuels into H_2 and CO in the anode. With the help of a catalyst, a chemical reaction takes place that generates an electron and a hydrogen ion. The electrolyte carries the positively charged ions while forcing negatively charged electron current to flow through a load, producing electricity. The electrolyte is the primary differentiator between fuel cells, and fuel cells are characterized by the type of electrolyte material.

times, but can deliver large amounts of power across several hours, often providing ten hours or more of capacity.

Though this technology holds great promise, the fuel cell industry remains marginal due to the high costs of commercialization of the product, high maintenance costs, and rapid degradation of stack efficiencies with respect to the theoretical potential. As a result, fuel cells continue to be labeled as the generation technology of the future.

Microgrid

Generation technologies are central to discussions around distributed energy systems. However, controls, infrastructure, and demand-side management are also an integral part of the broader discussion. The term 'microgrid' is used to refer to a smaller version of a main or central electrical grid that, much like its larger counterpart, consists of interconnected electrical loads and distributed energy generation resources that are typically controlled by a central control system. A microgrid may operate independently as its own self-contained entity, or may be interconnected with an adjoining central utility grid or neighboring microgrid.

The concept of the microgrid is often associated with a power system in developing countries where the centrally managed grid is weak or inadequate. However, microgrid architectures are deployed in the United States in various communities such as university campuses, hospitals, industry, and military. Fully 74 percent of the global microgrid market dollars were spent in North America in 2010.[37]

Although not a specific technology in itself, the notion of the microgrid is a system comprised of software, controls, and hardware infrastructure including sensors, inverters, switches, and converters. The microgrid and its primary components form the platform that is necessary for the integration of distributed generation resources with the local loads consuming the energy. The benefits of such architectures lie in the fact that they can be locally operated and controlled independently of a centrally managed utility. Such architecture enables distributed power systems, whether they operate on a stand-alone basis or as an integrated component of a larger central grid.

1.4 Functional Risks of DPS Technology

Despite the policy support and cost declines in technology, DPS applications are constrained by several fundamental technical and functional factors. These factors give rise to risks associated with power quality, "dispatchability," and reliability. Some of the most important technical risks of widespread DPS deployment and integration are listed below.

Power Quality

Some DPS technologies rely on power electronic devices, such as AC-to-DC or DC-to-AC converters. If such devices are not correctly set up, the integration of DPS power can result in a harmonic distortion and in operational difficulties to loads connected to the same distribution systems.[38]

Reactive Power Coordination

With the proper system configuration and network interface, DPS can bring relief to the power system by providing close-proximity power support at the distribution level. However, some renewable generation sources such as wind can worsen the reactive coordination problem. Wind generators have asynchronous induction generators designed for variable speed characteristics and, therefore, must rely on the network to which they are connected for reactive power support.[39]

Reliability and Reserve Margin

Intermittent power generation such as solar and wind is non-dispatchable. It is thus necessary to maintain sufficient generation reserve margins in order to provide reliable power generation. If there is a high level of distributed generation deployment, reserve margin adequacy can be a problem.

1.5 DPS Deployment Trends

In spite of these technical barriers to DPS, in 2007, there were an estimated 12 million distributed generation units installed across the United States, with a total capacity of more than 200 GW.[40] While distributed power systems include an array of technologies, the most notable areas of deployment have been in solar rooftop applications and CHP projects, with additional growth coming from other technologies such as fuel cells and grid storage technologies.

Solar Rooftop Installations

The Interstate Renewable Energy Council (IREC) estimates that in 2010 between 40 MW and 60 MW of off-grid solar power capacity was added across 50,000 sites, a 42 percent increase in the total number of sites from the year before.[41] A number of recently announced projects underscore the growth in distributed PV installations. In June 2011, ProLogis, one of the country's largest owners and operators of industrial real estate, in cooperation with NRG Energy and underwritten by Bank of America Merrill Lynch, announced that it had been granted a loan guarantee from the Department of Energy for a 733 MW distributed solar project. Known as "Project Amp," it will be the largest distributed solar power project in the country. NRG Energy will provide the initial financing while Bank of America may provide additional financing. The electricity generated will be sold into the grid and will not be used to power on-site buildings. Southern California Edison agreed to purchase the power generated by the first phase of the project, which may eventually be extended to as many as twenty-eight states and the District of Columbia.[42]

Also in June 2011, Google announced a $280 million investment in SolarCity, a Silicon Valley start-up, to help cover Solar-City's installation and maintenance costs. SolarCity's major initiative is SolarStrong, a $1 billion initiative to install rooftop solar panels on 160,000 private military residential and office buildings across 33 states. The project depended heavily on receiving a $344 million loan guarantee from the Department of Energy. At the time of writing, SolarCity was unable to meet the Energy Department's loan guarantee timeline, thus it has had to reduce the scale of SolarStrong by one-third.[43]

Combined Heat and Power (CHP)

Combined heat and power has been another area of distributed energy growth. A century-old technology, CHP accounts for 9 percent of U.S. electricity generation, most of which is natural-gas fired.[44] The major growth of CHP occurred after the enactment of PURPA in 1978, which prompted a 340 percent increase in installed CHP capacity from 1980 to 1993. Legislation passed by Congress in recent years—such as the Emergency Economic Stabilization Act of 2008 and the American Recovery and Reinvestment Act of 2009 (ARRA)—includes incentives for CHP development that promise further growth for the sector.[45] Examples of CHP incentive programs in these bills include a 10 percent investment tax credit for CHP plants, and roughly $100 million in grants for CHP and waste-heat recovery plants.[46] Also, in March 2011, the Department of Energy, in partnership with eight regional organizations, announced that it is looking to promote CHP projects in the U.S. Northwest, with the goal of increasing the efficiency of energy consumption in a number of sectors, including forestry processing and paper and pulp milling.[47] From 2005 to 2010, a total of 571 new CHP sites were added, amounting to a total electric capacity addition of 1,738 MW.

Due to differences in policies, incentives, and available natural resources at the state level, the growth of CHP has varied from state-to-state. Nearly half of all new CHP sites built between 2005 to 2010 were in California or New York. Texas, California, and Connecticut accounted for nearly 40 percent of all new installed CHP capacity built during the same time period.[48] State-level support looks to continue; in September 2011, California's Self-Generation Incentive Program (SGIP), a state-level program to promote distributed generation technologies, announced that natural gas-fired microturbines used in CHP projects would be eligible for SGIP assistance.[49]

Fuel Cells and Other Battery DPS Installations

Fuel cells are also gaining public interest as a significant driver of future DPS growth. Bloom Energy, a California-based company, has sold a number of its Bloom Energy Servers (or "Bloom Boxes" as they are known) to multinational corporations, including Google, Adobe, Bank of America, the Coca-Cola Company, FedEx, and Wal-Mart.

Another technology that is emerging as a potentially significant contributor to DPS penetration is grid storage. The Long Island Power Authority is currently considering a proposal from AES Energy Storage for a 400 MW battery-storage facility in lieu of traditional electricity generation sources. While the proposal is still at an early stage, AES already has an 8 MW lithium-ion battery system in operation in Johnson City, New York, and a 12 MW battery operation at its Los Andes site in Northern Chile, and is constructing a 32 MW facility to supplement the generation of the Laurel Mountain Wind Farm in Bellington, West Virginia.

Xcel Energy, a utility that provides electricity and natural gas services to states in the Midwest and West, is testing a 1 MW battery to store wind-generated electricity. The project, which consists of twenty 50 kW modules, will look to sell some of the stored electricity into the grid. The utility is also exploring the possibility of applying the same sodium-sulfur battery technology to storage of solar power. Other storage technology companies include A123, Beacon Power, Ice Energy Storage, Primus Power, and Xtreme Power.

Defense and Security DPS Applications

The U.S. Department of Defense is emerging as one of the major beneficiaries and users of DPS. DoD, whose energy consumption is roughly that of the state of Oregon, has recently signaled an increased interest in DPS, highlighted by the development of SolarCity's SolarStrong project. The military sees DPS as a way to diversify its electricity mix and bolster the security of its electricity infrastructure. Since 2007, the Nellis Air Force Base in Nevada has been powered by the country's largest PV array of more than 72,000 solar panels.[50] Ten years before that, the Navy built a 270 MW geothermal power plant to power the China Lake Naval Air Weapons Station in southern California.[51] Recently, microgrids have received a lot of interest from DoD and, with assistance from corporations such as General Electric and Lockheed Martin, the department is implementing microgrids across its bases. In July 2009, GE announced that it was awarded $2 million in Federal stimulus funding from DoD to implement a smart microgrid demonstration project at the Twentynine Palms Base in California, the world's largest Marine Corps Base.[52] According to Dorothy Robyn, deputy undersecretary of defense for installations and environment, microgrids "allow us to operate more efficiently . . . in a normal mode but [also to] facilitate the incorporation of solar, wind, [and] other forms of renewable energy . . . . And most important, if the grid goes down it will allow us to prioritize and continue to operate activities that are most critical."[53]

Expert Forum

DPS technologies are inherently local; what works in one place may not work in another. This means that, even more than with conventional centralized energy systems, DPS viability is subject to local needs and conditions. Conference participants highlighted the importance of understanding local electricity market conditions when evaluating DPS suitability and suggested a strategy of focusing on particular geographic regions to reduce DPS deployment costs.

On differences in local conditions

"We're very close in terms of the economics of distributed generation. . . . [Economic viability] depends on whether or not you're able to locate the distributed generation in a congested node area, which means that you have the benefit of avoiding the distribution and transmission, capacity build-out, the additional generation build-out."

—Amy Guy Wagner, *Senior Consultant, E3*

"There is a huge delta between the prices of electricity in different regions of the country. In North Carolina, we're about 30 percent below the national average, while in California they're about 30 percent above the national average. So what works in one market is different from another just based on price alone."

—James Rogers, *Chairman, President, and Chief Executive Officer, Duke Energy*

DPS technologies, taken individually, are limited in scale and scope. For example, technical, climatic, and market viability is generally more narrowly defined than with conventional alternatives. But taken together, DPS implementations offer a wealth of choice such that particular technology combinations can be suited to match those niche conditions where centralized power systems might be too inflexible.

Key issues identified by conference participants that affect DPS locally-specific viability include:

- Special end-user needs such as high service uptime or backup capability, inflexible peak-time electricity demand, fuel choice flexibility requirements, or image and marketability;
- Natural conditions affecting specific DPS technologies such as solar incidence, wind or hydrologic resource, ambient temperature, seasonal effects, or fuel supply chains;
- The characteristics of DPS substitutes such as differences in regional grid prices, node or time-of-day congestion, or rural service availability;
- Differences in local regulatory frameworks such as permitting cost and capacity, rate design, or utility acceptance;
- The ability and experience of private sector DPS enablers such as project developers, financiers, or maintenance providers.

On the strategy of regional DPS development zones

"You really can't do one by one. There's a fundamental difference between trying to do one 1,000 MW project and trying to do one thousand 1 MW projects. Suddenly, when you're doing the interconnection queue you have to look at the cluster. Otherwise, if you do one by one and then someone changes the location or their size, it has this ripple effect. So you have to really start looking at zones."

—Robert Weisenmiller, *Chairman, California Energy Commission*

"More than half of the U.S. population is packed into a few dozen metro areas. Distributed power systems have a real potential for impacting those areas."

—Bradley Schoener, *Energy Portfolio Manager,*
The MITRE Corporation

Because of the location-specific attributes of DPS, some panelists suggested that an efficient way to move DPS deployment from niche cases to broader uptake is to encourage the development of particular zones that might already have DPS-friendly natural, operational, and economic conditions and where supportive and consistent policy frameworks could be established to incentivize private investment. The goal of this strategy would be to reduce total system transaction cost, timeframe, and risk for DPS deployment while, through economies of scale, helping to bring down the overhead per DPS unit within that zone. Ideal DPS zones may, however, look quite different from one another—ranging from rural electrification zones, to urban areas, to military installations.

CHAPTER 2

ECONOMIC AND ENVIRONMENTAL COST-BENEFIT ANALYSIS OF DPS

2.1 Costs and Benefits of Distributed Generation

In this chapter we review the best currently available information on the costs of small distributed generation and compare it to the costs of generating and delivering power with the current central-station system. The comparison relies on standard utility practice for comparing resource costs. The results reflect the answers state commissions and utility analysts are likely to produce, and the analysis is useful as a current benchmark. Consistent with typical industry practice, the costs and benefits include only "monetizable" values. Those costs and benefits that are hard to quantify such as health effects, decreased environmental impacts, and security benefits are discussed in subsequent chapters.

The costs of distributed generation are expressed as the Levelized Cost of Energy (LCOE) which includes capital costs, fuel, maintenance, financing and all other distributed generation costs. The costs are then compared to the "benefits" of having installed distributed generation. We compute "benefits" as "avoided costs": those costs the electric utility would spend generating and delivering the same electricity in the absence of the distributed generator. This is a "Total Resource Cost" comparison to determine whether central generation or distributed generation costs less overall and is not the same comparison a factory owner might make which relies on the utility retail rate.

The result is that while the gap between DPS and central station generation is shrinking, distributed power generation is still not cost competitive in most cases.[1] Recent large gains in the cost-competitiveness of solar photovoltaics (PV) in part driven by a massive investment in Germany and other European countries, has generated excitement, predominantly in California but also on both the West and East Coasts where the avoided costs are generally higher. Fuel cells and microturbines have made significant technological progress as well and provide promise for capturing smaller-scale combined heat and power applications.

All of these technologies have growing markets, particularly since they all have retail applications aided by rules such as Net Energy Metering (NEM) available in many states that allow utility customers to "run the meter backwards," incentive programs such as the California Solar Initiative (CSI), and other subsidies such as federal investment tax credits. As markets grow, costs are likely to decline further. However, it remains a question whether or when DPS will close the gap completely. The industry will have to maintain steady declines in costs before DPS are competitive with the costs of central generation.

Cost of Distributed Generation—Levelized Cost of Energy

Levelized cost of energy (LCOE) is a commonly-used metric that compares the cost per unit of energy (MWh) across different technology types. This metric translates up-front capital costs, ongoing expenditures, taxes, and resource performance factors into a levelized, life-cycle energy cost that takes into account changes in costs and production over time. Formulaically, the LCOE refers to the present value of the life-cycle costs of a project divided by the present value of its life-cycle energy production.

$$LCOE = \frac{PV\ (\text{Life-cycle Costs})}{PV\ (\text{MWh Energy Production})}$$

It is important to define a comparative cost metric such as LCOE in a rigorous way in order to avoid unintentionally introducing bias into the technology-specific results. For example, a model that fails to account for financing realities such as a minimum debt service coverage ratio (DSCR) required by lenders may unduly favor capital-intensive technologies. Therefore, the LCOE model used incorporates a minimum DSCR and many other factors in order to provide a realistic unbiased comparison across technologies. The levelized cost analysis used for this analysis is fully documented and publicly available.[2]

For the present analysis, capital and operating costs, capacity factors, and tax treatment for all of the distributed technologies (with the exception of solar PV) were taken from the best available public sources.[3] All of the input assumptions and results by cost component for each scenario are provided in Annex 1. An ITRON SGIP study provides a robust review of distributed generation technology, cost, and performance. For the PV technologies, we use capital and operating costs, capacity factors, and tax treatment equivalent to the recent data published in the California Solar Initiative Cost-Effectiveness Report (for smaller projects) and E3's 33 percent Renewable Costing Analysis completed for the California Long-Term Procurement Plan.

The financing assumptions are provided in Table 2.1. The assumptions were validated with debt and equity providers and

TABLE 2.1 LCOE Financing Assumptions

Input	Assumption
Percent Financed with Equity	See note *
After-Tax WACC	8.25 percent
Debt Interest Rate	7.50 percent
Cost of Equity	Function of WACC, interest rate, percent equity
Target Minimum DSCR	1.40
Debt Period in Years	20
Federal Tax Rate	35 percent
State Tax Rate	8.84 percent
Tax Credit Rate	30 percent

* The model minimizes the percent equity constrained to a target average DSCR of 1.40

vetted through public stakeholder proceedings at the California Public Utility Commission.[4] The LCOE model applies the same Weighted Average Cost of Capital (WACC) and cost of debt across all technologies. The model then solves for the minimum equity required to maintain a DSCR of 1.40. The model also assumes that the project developer can take full advantage of all available state and federal tax incentives and depreciation. In this way, the model finds the most favorable project finance structure for each technology, thus providing an equal comparison basis.

Benefits of Distributed Generation—Avoided Costs

Quantified benefits include all of the costs that would have been incurred by the utility without the distributed generation in place. That is, the cost of generating and delivering the electricity to the customer with the conventional system. These quantified benefits are also known as "avoided costs" and include generation costs (energy and capacity), avoided or deferred transmission and distribution (T&D) capacity investments, and ancillary services such as reserves and regulation.

The avoided costs of a distributed generator are area- and time-specific. That is, they can vary significantly according to where the distributed generation is located, the shape of its output profile, and its reliability. In general, there are two categories of avoided costs: energy and capacity. Energy includes the avoided fuel and maintenance in the central generator as well as losses over the T&D lines to deliver the power. Capacity includes any avoided infrastructure investment such as additional power plants and T&D lines. In particular, the capacity avoided costs are sensitive to the output profile and reliability of the distributed generation on the system. Since the utility system is sized so that it can serve peak load reliably, if utility planners do not see a peak load reduction or cannot count on a peak reduction because the distributed generation is unreliable, then they will continue to make infrastructure investments and capacity savings will be zero.

Figure 2.1 compares a range of avoided costs for coal and natural gas regions in the United States showing a low value of approximately $25/MWh representing only energy, and a high value of $120/MWh representing avoided energy plus avoided new coal power plant, transmission, and distribution infrastructure as well.[5] The distributed generation's benefits would be at least $25/ MWh almost regardless of when it operated and where it was located. To capture the capacity value it would have to be operating during the peak, and to capture the T&D capacity

FIGURE 2.1 AVOIDED COST COMPARISON

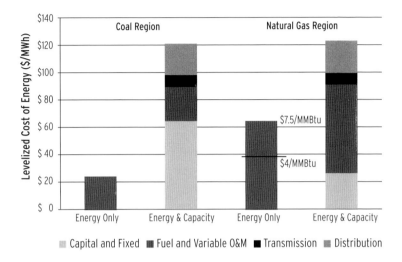

value the distributed generation would have to be located in a constrained portion of the utility grid and avoid upgrades.

The low end of the avoided cost spectrum in each region represents the base energy value with little or no additional T&D or capacity components. Such a value may be appropriate for resources which are non-coincident with peak load, such as wind energy which often produces power during evening hours. The higher value is based on avoidance of significant T&D investment and capital and fixed costs associated with the need to build new plants. Thus, when comparing the distributed resource to the avoided cost, it is critical to ask whether or not the resource can provide peak power, as a significant amount of the avoided cost may come from avoided T&D capacity and peak generation capacity. This means that to achieve maximum avoided cost value, the distributed system must be located close to load at a congested node which would otherwise require a transmission or distribution upgrade. For the natural gas region, the energy value is shown assuming a low natural gas price of $4/MMBtu which reflects continued low gas prices perhaps from shale gas, and a higher price of $7.50/MMBtu which reflects higher prices and restricted or limited impact from shale gas.

2.2 Results of Cost-Benefit Comparison

Figure 2.2 shows the comparison of the LCOE of a range of distributed generation technologies to the regional coal and natural gas avoided costs. The minimum avoided cost is about $25/MWh in coal regions, which is representative of the energy cost of coal. For the natural gas region, the minimum is about $40/MWh reflecting low natural gas price. The high end of the avoided cost spectrum is similar, based on displacement of either natural gas or coal-fired generation and includes capital and fixed costs for new power plant construction as well as higher avoided T&D capacity costs and a higher gas price. To achieve this level of benefit, a generator would need to produce energy during peak hours in a location with planned T&D capacity investments and be located in an area without excess generation capacity.

The distributed resources that are competitive with the high end of the current avoided cost of the centralized coal and gas generation are gas turbines and IC engines with CHP. Both large and community-scale wind applications are also competitive with the higher range of central station generation; however, these applications are difficult to locate in areas where they are able to provide high capacity and grid support value. Among solar projects, large applications (5–20 MW) are also close to cost competitiveness. At the low-end of the coal avoided-cost spectrum (based on use of existing coal plants and

FIGURE 2.2 E3 Analysis of Economics of DG Compared to Avoided Cost Range[6]

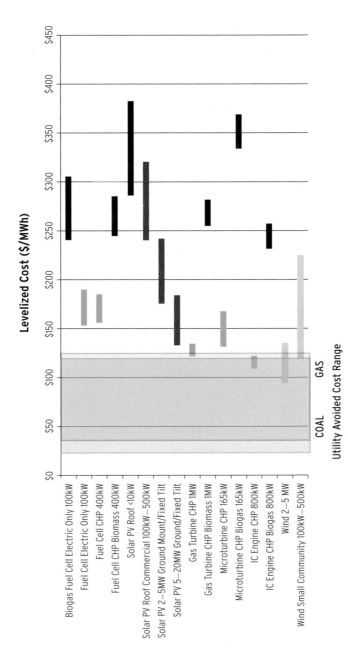

low T&D avoided costs) none of the technologies is as of yet cost-effective.

Fossil fuel-fired generators that can capture waste heat to provide hot water and steam remain the cost-effective options to expand distributed resource penetration they have since the 1970s. This is not the utopian vision of the new distributed resource system that many envisage. Fossil fuel-based resources have environmental attributes which are particularly troublesome near heavily populated load centers, where avoided power is generally most valuable. What is new—and a development that may reflect a paradigm shift in the next decade if cost trends continue—is that solar PV is near the top end of the range. Since solar is very modular and can be effectively constructed from very small to large sizes it can be targeted to capture high value locations. The California Public Utilities Commission (PUC) has proposed a program that would offer a feed-in tariff (FIT) to target small renewable generators like photovoltaics in the parts of the grid where they capture the most value.

Cost of Carbon

The benefits and costs in Figure 2.2 do not include the costs of carbon. There is no consensus opinion on when or how carbon dioxide emissions will begin to be priced in the United States in the future. However, a comprehensive cap-and-trade bill has been debated in Congress and the EPA does have regulatory authority over CO_2 emissions. In this section we assess whether a price on carbon can fundamentally change the distributed generation equation.

Figure 2.3 shows the same comparison of costs and benefits if the costs of CO_2 are "moderate." That is, near the levels projected from prior cap-and-trade legislation at roughly \$30/ton CO_2.

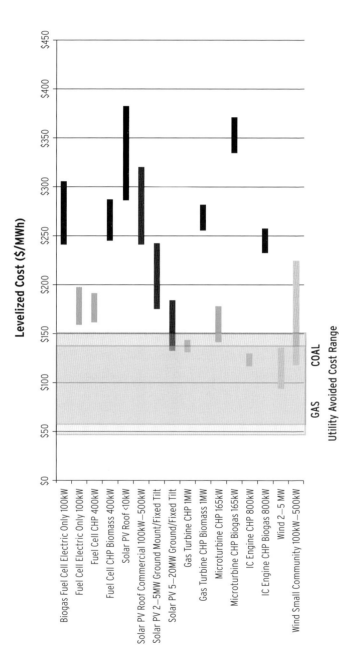

FIGURE 2.3 Economics of DG Compared to Avoided Costs with $30/ton CO$_2$ Cost

Relative to Figure 2.2, the avoided costs in Figure 2.3 are higher, reflecting the addition of a carbon price to the generation cost. The avoided costs of coal increase by more than those of gas, reflecting the greater carbon emissions of coal per unit of power produced. Fossil fuel-burning distributed generation also increases in cost when carbon is priced. The gas-fired DPS technologies in Figure 2.3 show a higher cost range than in Figure 2.2. Clean renewable technologies, however, do not increase in cost and thus become more cost-effective relative to utility avoided costs.

However, even with carbon price included, the fundamental picture of DPS economics is unchanged. Fossil-fueled distributed generation with combined heat and power applications can be cost-effective; solar and wind become more competitive. The major change with even a 'moderate' carbon price is a shift in utility generation from coal to natural gas. For DPS, even with inclusion of carbon costs, costs will need to fall further before they are cost-effective as an alternative to central station generation in most applications.

Expert Forum

"The last big transformation [in the utility sector] was deregulation which, you may recall from the 1990s, led to a lot of hoopla. . . . It led to a lot of power plants being built, 200 GW of competitive power plants being built without putting ratepayers at risk anywhere. . . . That's going to look like a minor, minor preview of what's going to happen in the next decade or so as the costs of distributed generation and distributive power systems come down and the costs of regulated utility rates go up."

—Steve Corneli, *Senior Vice President, Sustainability, Policy, and Strategy, NRG Energy*

Conference participants noted that while it is important for investors and regulators to understand the current cost competitiveness of DPS applications, they must also consider how that cost calculus may change into the future. Otherwise, with the emerging DPS market outpacing regulatory action, today's reasonable policy could become tomorrow's roadblock. In addition to potential regulatory action around carbon dioxide emissions that could change electricity generation costs, key dynamics identified to this end include rapidly falling prices for some DPS products and the likelihood of rising utility rates. A third issue was cost implications from the unresolved debate around the external impacts of DPS on future electricity distribution system investment requirements.

On the impact to DPS deployment if prices rapidly fall

"The projected price of the trend line in solar PV is eating through this twenty-cent competitive with all-in rates, heading for the twelve-cent, fifteen-cent, competitive with energy only costs. . . . So, if we don't deal with this issue now when people are incentivized to bypass the transmission and distribution system, we're going to have to deal with it in a few years when they're incentivized to bypass the whole darn thing. . . . When do we start actually gearing up for that policy discussion and how do we do that?"

—Ken Colburn, *Senior Associate, Regulatory Assistance Project*

"Tomorrow, when these things get even cheaper, consumers will be saying, 'What do you mean I can't put it on my roof if the policies aren't there? What do you mean I can't put something that costs ten cents a kWh on my roof when my utility rate is twenty cents?' And that's going to be a very big, big driver that I think we're not really anticipating enough as a country."

—Steve Corneli, *Senior Vice President, Sustainability, Policy, and Strategy, NRG Energy*

As solar PV panel manufacturing capacity grows and cost per watt falls, some panelists argued that we are near a tipping point where residential and commercial end-users will elect to install rooftop systems in mass numbers (driven more by the economics of doing so rather than ideology or other preferences). Others, however, pointed to the relatively stable costs of installation, labor, and balance-of-system components that now make up a major portion of final system costs, and that these would be difficult to substantially reduce. Others identified the temporary oversupply conditions in panel manufacturing to argue that PV system costs may not fall as fast as anticipated. If prices do continue to fall and uptake is rapid, there are concerns that the current deficiencies in immature state regulatory policy or inadequate distribution infrastructure may be painfully revealed.

On the impact to DPS deployment if utility rates rise

"You're going to see the real price of electricity in this country rise over the next several decades in stark contrast to the past fifty years when the real price of electricity has been flat."

—James Rogers, *Chairman, President, and Chief Executive Officer, Duke Energy*

Some industry stakeholders expect the cost of providing electricity services—and therefore end-user electric rates—to rise in the United States over the coming years. Reasons for the rise include: potential gains in natural gas prices from current lows that have resulted from over-investment in domestic fracking capacity; new or stricter federal regulations on sulfur, mercury, particulate, and carbon dioxide emissions from conventional fossil baseload generators; new safety regulations and high financing costs for extending, replacing, or expanding large-scale nuclear power generation; and increased costs to site new transmission capacity, relieve peak node congestion, or upgrade grid communications infrastructure.

Others point out that U.S. electricity demand is experiencing slow rates of growth as end-use efficiency improves and therefore new large scale generation capacity may not need to be built, or that natural gas prices can be expected to remain low as domestic supply expands; both of these would suppress potential cost growth. If rates do rise for these DPS "substitutes," however, that could provide a cost umbrella to enable the economic deployment of DPS products that might not otherwise be commercially viable.

On the unresolved cost impact of DPS on electricity distribution infrastructure

"It's a risk, and commissions are used to calibrating risks. Lots of variables, I understand, but zero is the wrong answer, and this is a risk. Let's run scenarios, let's figure out what the right number is in this state at this time."

—Ken Colburn, *Senior Associate, Regulatory Assistance Project*

"Lose the idea that all electricity is the same. . . . It's extremely difficult to figure out what the delivered cost is and where it's coming from, but we know the answer's not zero . . . and we're penalizing the technologies that are distributed by trying to compare them with the baseload and ignoring this thing."

—Tom Casten, *Chairman, Recycled Energy Development*

"You're going to start running into rate and cost issues. One of the things we're finding, we have now about 3,000 MW of distributed generation in the California system. That's out of a roughly 60,000 MW system. . . . We're starting to get to the point of having real impacts on our system, certainly on our gas loads. . . . What happens when you suddenly discover your loads in the afternoon are dropping off because of PV production; what's the implication of that?"

—Robert Weisenmiller, *Chairman, California Energy Commission*

"We've participated in a number of studies addressing these sorts of economic concerns and we've been able to show, when you really drill down on this issue, that oftentimes the subsidy does not flow from nonparticipating rate pairs to customers who install distributed generation but it actually flows back the opposite way."

—Kevin Fox, *Interstate Renewable Energy Council*

The direction and magnitude of the externality assumed when deploying DPS within an existing electricity distribution system has not been settled, let alone internalized into market dynamics. But while most conference participants agreed that this externality is "non-zero," since there is not a widely agreed-upon figure, the default "zero" persists in cost calculations.

There are two main dynamics at play in this issue: existing U.S. electricity distribution systems were not designed to accommodate DPS, and these systems are aging or at capacity in many regions and so require upgrade. The impact of deploying DPS on top of these existing systems is very much monetary in that costs are real and immediate, but it is also often external or distributional in that the installer or end-user of a piece of DPS hardware such as rooftop PV may, without compensation, both benefit from and contribute to the broader distribution system that supports it.

In the short-term or narrow sense then, DPS seem to levy an external cost upon existing distribution systems with the need for supporting investment in smart metering, enhanced neighborhood-scale transformer infrastructure, and utility dispatch or load management. More broadly and over time, however, the distributed generation and storage offered by DPS may offset otherwise needed investments in expensive new long-distance transmission, central generation infrastructure, or peaking management and other grid services. Exactly what these costs and benefits are, where they fall, and how they will be accounted for vary by location.

CHAPTER 3

SECURITY-RELATED BENEFITS OF DPS

The economic analysis in Chapter 2 assessed the costs and benefits of DPS relative to centralized generation using a standard cost-comparison model based on quantifiable inputs. This chapter attempts to assess one of the non-quantified aspects of DPS: their value to energy security. For the purposes of this paper, energy security is divided into two categories:

- The security of the civilian grid with respect to intentional or unintentional disruption; and
- The provision of energy to the U.S. military, both at domestic facilities and in front-line deployments.

3.1 Energy Security and the Civilian Grid

Security and reliability of supply

The U.S. economy is increasingly dependent on reliable electricity. The rapid computerization of many industry sectors such as health care, banking, and commerce has resulted in an enormous increase in the need for reliable power. Between 2006 and 2011, the power consumption of all computer servers is estimated to increase from 61 billion kWh to 100 billion kWh.[1] Such an increase has added to the pressures on already stressed transmission infrastructure.[2]

Electricity delivery is reliable only when supply perfectly matches demand. A perfectly reliable system would therefore be operating 8760 hours a year, 24 hours a day, 365 days a year. Power-system reliability is measured in levels of "9"s. Table 3.1 illustrates the length of outages associated with different levels of reliability.[3]

According to the Galvin Electricity Initiative, the U.S. power sector is designed to run at a reliability of "three nines"—i.e. 99.9 percent, far lower than the Japanese grid with its "five nines" reliability.[4] Costs of disruption to the power system are estimated to be as high as $80 billion annually.[5] Of this, 73 percent, or $53 billion, is from losses in the commercial sector and 25 percent, or $20 billion, in the industrial sector.[6] The estimate for residential losses is $1.5 billion, or only about 2 percent of the total.

TABLE 3.1 GRID RELIABILITY AND OUTAGE DURATION

Reliability	Yearly Outage Duration
99 percent	3.65 days
99.9 percent	8.77 hours
99.99 percent	52.5 minutes
99.999 percent	5.25 minutes
99.9999 percent	30 seconds
99.99999 percent	3 seconds

There are two main causes for system outages:

1. capacity deficiencies
2. faults and failures

Capacity deficiencies are interruptions deliberately deployed when demand exceeds supply and refer to (i) inadequate supply of power to meet market demand, (ii) an inadequate contingent supply of electricity for an unexpected event.[7]

Faults and failures refer to events over which utilities have little or no control. **Faults** are short circuits in the transmission or distribution systems that are caused by an external event, such as contact with trees or animals, or lightning strikes. **Failures** refer to outages due to human error or equipment malfunction, usually in high-voltage bushings, transformer windings, or surge arrestors.[8] Around 94 percent of all outages occur due to faults and failures, most of which happen in the distribution system.[9] Outages are short, but have a widespread impact.[10]

The burdens on the centralized power system are compounded by requirements to integrate large-scale sources of renewable generation often located far from demand centers: twenty-nine states have so far enacted renewable portfolio standards (RPS) that require utilities to generate a minimum amount of their output using renewable sources. In order to connect with the (mostly urban) load centers, this renewable generation capacity will require the construction of new transmission lines. Cost projections for the necessary level of transmission construction range between $60 and $100 billion over the next ten years.[11] In a straitened economic climate, such sums are unlikely to be made available by the public sector. The result is likely to be more pressure on an already overburdened grid infrastructure, with detrimental consequences for reliability. Without commercially available energy storage or other technical solutions, this high

---

Reliability Metrics

Electric power system reliability is measured both on a local and regional basis. *Local distribution system reliability performance* typically is measured using industry-accepted statistics that measure the frequency and duration of sustained interruptions to electricity consumers. These are referred to as System Average Interruption Frequency Index (SAIFI) and System Average Interruption Duration Index (SAIDI), respectively.

On a regional basis, reliability is measured by the *loss-of-load probability (LOLP)* metric. LOLP is a function of the generation and peak load, however, it does not include any failures in the T&D systems. Loss-of-load probability characterizes the adequacy of generation to serve the load on the system. It does not model the reliability of the transmission and distribution system where most outages occur. Although based upon a probabilistic analysis of the generating resources and the peak loads, the LOLP is not really a probability. Rather, it is an expected value calculated on either an hourly or daily basis. A typical LOLP is "one day in ten years" or "0.1 days in a year." This is often misinterpreted as a probability of 0.1 that there will be an outage in a given year. Loss-of-load probability characterizes the adequacy of generation to serve the load on the system. It does not model the reliability of the transmission and distribution system where most outages occur.

---

influx of intermittent resources is also likely to present reliability challenges.

Security and the Smart Grid

The smart grid is a concept that aims to combine the benefits of information technology with new and existing energy generation and storage technologies to deliver a more efficient, flexible power infrastructure. As envisioned by the Department of

Energy (DOE) in the 2007 Energy Security and Independence Act, the smart grid will enable the "dynamic optimization of grid operations" through the integration of "smart" meters and consumer appliances that are able to automate power consumption, as well as the development of two-way communication between energy providers and end-users. In DOE's view, the implementation of the smart grid also includes increased penetration of DPS. Certain elements of the smart grid are intended to improve the security of the current power infrastructure. Through the receipt of real-time data from smart meters and other sensors on the system, utilities will be able to identify the location of an outage more easily and, therefore, restore service more quickly than with the current system. Utilities will also be able to monitor real-time electricity consumption, giving them the ability to better manage the system in periods of high demand.

However, the introduction of digital controls into the electric grid also comes with the potential for two new kinds of security threat. First, by relying on a complex set of computerized controls for the management of the electric system, the smart grid exposes generation, transmission, and distribution assets to a range of prospective failures or malfunctions at those control points.

Second, by providing online access to vital infrastructure controls, the smart grid is likely to open a new avenue of possible attack to prospective saboteurs. Cybersecurity is a serious and growing global challenge and smart grid applications have been identified by many as providing "new vectors for attack."[12] This challenge is increased by the growing commoditization of the hardware and software used in the control and management of the power system. According to the National Defense University, the Supervisory Control and Data Acquisition (SCADA) systems used for the control and distribution of electric power, water, pipelines, and nuclear power-plants are increasingly being managed by Internet-based technologies[13] and commercial off-the-shelf switches, routers, and operating systems.[14]

Analysis of outages due to computer failure shows that to date disruptions from unintended actions have been more common than intentional attacks. A nuclear power plant was shut down in Georgia in 2008 for forty-eight hours due to a mistake in controlling software systems: an inconsistency in software design that was uploaded to a computer resulted in safety systems registering this glitch as a lack of data, which usually happens when there is a drop in water reservoirs that cool the fuel rods. Though unintentional, this shut-down of the power plant cost the utility about a $1 million a day for purchasing additional fuels on the spot market. Another example of a shut-down due to a cyber event occurred at Browns Ferry nuclear power plant in Alabama in 2006, after two recirculation pumps failed due to a flood of computer data traffic known as a "data storm."[15] While cyber-attacks on the power system have not caused such major outages in the United States to date, the potential for large-scale disruption has been highlighted by demonstrations such as Idaho National Lab's 2007 Aurora Generator Test, in which physical damage was caused to a generator through exploitation of a safety flaw in a SCADA system.

The Security Potential for DPS

DPS have the potential to increase the security of the civilian grid in two main ways: through relieving pressure constraints on the existing transmission and distribution system, thereby decreasing the chances of a reliability disruption; and through diversifying the sources of generation, making the power system less vulnerable to an attack or a failure at points in the centralized grid. The avoided costs of greater reliability disruptions due to system constraints and system outages resulting from an attack are difficult to quantify. The ability of DPS to mitigate these costs also needs to be weighed against the extent to which distributed applications *increase* system vulnerability by replacing baseload generation capacity with a diffuse array of small scale sources and by opening up more potential points of attack into the grid. Given the likelihood of unprecedented pressures on the power system, and the emergence of the smart grid with all its attendant costs and benefits, the extent to which DPS can mitigate security vulnerability to the civilian grid should be added into an assessment of their value.

3.2 Energy Security in the U.S. Military

The U.S. military has substantial concerns about the security and reliability of the current centralized energy system. These concerns manifest themselves in two ways: the first relates to the security of military installations on the grid and the ability of those installations to effectively island themselves from the grid when necessary; the second relates to expeditionary energy—or the ability of the military to use various distributed energy technologies at forward operating bases or other locations within the combat theater.

Motivated by soaring fuel and electricity costs, the U.S. Department of Defense (DoD) has increasingly recognized the importance of energy security to its strategy, as seen by the increase to DoD's budget on energy security issues from $400 million to $1.2 billion over the past five years.[16]

Military Installations

The DoD has a substantial portfolio of real estate, including more than 500,000 buildings totaling nearly 2.2 billion square feet, approximately three times the total square footage occupied by the world's Wal-Marts.[17] Once seen simply as staging areas, bases have now become increasingly mission-critical as was demonstrated during Hurricane Katrina, when much of the relief effort was carried out from military bases. The Department of Homeland Security has also developed plans to have military bases be a key point of response in the event of a major terrorist incident. Given their new roles, the supply of uninterruptible, secure power to these facilities is now a necessity.[18] In the view of the military, the assurance of such supply is not possible through sole reliance on the civilian power grid. As a 2008 DoD report noted: "Critical national security and homeland defense missions are at an unacceptably high risk of extended outage from failure of the grid."[19] The report recommended that the military "reduce the risk to critical missions at fixed installations from loss of commercial power and other critical national infrastructure."

Military concerns over power disruption extend beyond bases themselves. The prospect of an extended outage to defense production equipment suppliers—either through unintentional disruption or through cyber-attacks such as that in September 2011 on Mitsubishi, the Japanese government's largest arms supplier—present an additional serious and credible threat. Iran famously was set back for several years by the Stuxnet worm, which badly crippled Iran's nuclear capability.[20] According to senior military officials interviewed for this study, there are concerns that a similar attack in the United States could cripple U.S. military capabilities.

Combat Theater

The U.S. military consumes 360,000 barrels of oil per day, almost as much as Pakistan and Thailand and slightly more than the Philippines.[21] While more than 80 percent of that consumption is for jet fuel, a substantial portion is also used for electricity in portable generators, making the military one of the few primary users of oil for the electric grid. The current costs of that fuel are high; they are also difficult to estimate reliably, especially when one includes, as the military does, the so-called "fully-burdened" costs of fuel that include all of the ancillary costs of delivering and maintaining reliable fuel supplies where they are needed. Even without such calculations, the U.S. military pays an enormous amount for fuel: $8.8 billion for 130 million barrels of petroleum in 2005 and $17.9 billion for 134 million barrels of oil in 2008.

While the costs of liquid fuels have little bearing on power generation in the civilian sector, this is less true in the military where a significant amount of liquid fuel is used to power diesel generators during wartime. The military currently deploys approximately 125,000 diesel generators and, according to one fully-burdened cost of fuel estimate, the costs for operating these generators is between $3.5 and $5 billion annually during wartime,[22] during which they are the army's largest consumers of fuel.

The costs of fuel use for front-line power generation also have to take into consideration the supply chains required to deliver it. Supply convoys are the key point of vulnerability in the military energy security infrastructure and it is estimated that there is one casualty for every forty-six resupply convoys in Afghanistan. The troops in Afghanistan need about 897 refueling missions a year, indicating that casualties associated with

TABLE 3.2 USAGE OF FOSSIL FUEL-BASED
DISTRIBUTED ENERGY INCREASES DRAMATICALLY
DURING WARTIME

Source	Peacetime	Wartime
Combat Vehicles	30	162
Combat Aircraft	144	307
Tactical Vehicles	44	173
Generators	26	357
Non-Tactical	51	51
Total	295	1050

Source: Report of the Defense Science Board Task
Force on DoD Energy Strategy, 2008.

supplying them can be expected to result in the death or injury
of around twenty soldiers a year.[23]

While the fully-burdened costs of fuel can vary dramatically depending upon the assumptions— such as the location of
fuel within the combat space—situational cost estimates show
that many specialized forays into combat can routinely require
hundreds of dollars per gallon. Even relatively routine activities,
such as on-board fueling of a ship away from combat zones, can
require substantially higher fuel costs than the retail costs. Thus,
the cost of fuel, while technically "only" in the low tens of billions, can dramatically expand when other factors are taken into
consideration.[24] This cost, both in terms of fuel requirements
and human casualties, represents the true cost of distributed
energy to the military.

As Army Secretary John McHugh noted in an August 2011
speech, the average soldier during WWII used just one gallon of
fuel per day. Today, in Iraq and Afghanistan, the average soldier
consumes fifteen to twenty-two gallons of fuel per day.[25] Thus,

having secure and stable energy sources is a critical goal for the modern military.

The need for power on the front lines also has a direct impact on the operational abilities of soldiers on the ground. About 15–20 percent of the average marine's packweight of seventy to ninety pounds now consists of batteries (used to charge everything from night-vision goggles to radios to laptops), substantially reducing mobility.[26] Moreover, the DoD projects the weight of batteries, for a three-day foot patrol, to increase to eighteen pounds per soldier by 2012, up from approximately ten pounds in 2010.[27] This implies that, with a seventy-pound packweight, batteries would make up one-fourth of the weight.

The Role for DPS

DPS have the potential to play a large role in the provision of secure energy for the military, both at its bases and in theater. Powering systems through distributed generation is one method of islanding key military systems to reduce vulnerability to attacks. DoD has recognized this, and seeks to increase its use of distributed energy, including new forms of non-fossil distributed energy, to power its facilities. DoD plans to spend over $600 million in fuel cells alone from 2008 to 2013.[28]

The integration of DPS into military base electrical infrastructure is a logical choice: many of these bases have a robust electrical infrastructure that is self-contained with on-site personnel capable of operating and maintaining the complex systems necessarily for the provision of a higher level of electrical security. The 2008 DoD report cited above called for an immediate islanding of several military installations, though the specific locations were classified and not listed in the published report.[29]

A military base represents an ideal environment for security-enhanced microgrid applications, one where the electric infrastructure can either operate independently or be integrated with the larger electric grid. This already occurs on many military bases where back-up generators provide a back-up supply to the broader electric utility supply in the event of an interruption.[30] The military accounted for an estimated 15 percent of the U.S. microgrid market in 2010.[31]

Smart systems are likely to have a key role in DPS operations in a microgrid environment as stand-alone, self-healing systems are likely to become essential during major disruptions of supply when the attention of military personnel is devoted to other duties.[32] DoD spent more than $190 million in smart grid applications in 2010, indicating a substantially enhanced awareness of smart grid benefits. DPS resources, where limited or interrupted by events, may need to be redirected to mission-critical lines.

DPS also have significant potential role for the military in the combat theater, particularly as a means of reducing the amount of liquid fuel and battery capacity required for power generation.

The Marine Experimental Forward Operating Base at Quantico, VA, was deployed in 2010 as a way to test new and emerging technologies that will allow for better and more mobile deployment of security forces. Among the most prominent technologies tested were flexible solar technologies that can be deployed as part of tents on forward operating bases. These "solar tents" were used to power computers, radios, and other key electronics while working silently, thus eliminating potential noise signals from generators that could alert insurgents to a military presence. The solar tents had up to 2 kW of rooftop power, representing about one-third of the power of an average residential solar system installed in the United States in 2010.[33] As a result of successful domestic tests, marines from the India Company 3rd Battalion 5th Marine Regiment have deployed the technology in Afghanistan. The successful deployment included a three-week foot patrol where 700 pounds of weight were saved, as the need for a battery resupply was eliminated, as well as the operation of two patrol bases on 100 percent renewable energy. As a result, the Marine Corps has made the decision to replicate this capability for all of their bases in the restive Helmand province.[34]

Meanwhile, a new Rucksack Enhanced Portable Power System (REPPS) developed for the army includes a rollable solar charging mat as well as rechargeable batteries and fuel-cell chargers for powering radios, laptops and other devices. Currently weighing approximately nine pounds, future iterations promise substantial weight savings. Recently, 725 of these systems were delivered to troops in Afghanistan.[35]

3.3 Summary

For both civilian and military dimensions, a decentralization of electricity infrastructure can allow for a more secure and reliable generation of electricity primarily by reducing the reliance on traditional centralized generation facilities. On the civilian side, increasing the penetration of DPS means that consumers are less vulnerable to an electrical outage. Such outages can occur due to technical issues such as grid failures or capacity shortfalls, or because of deliberate attacks—either physical or cyber-related—on the power grid. On the defense side, DoD has expressed keen interest in using DPS to increase energy security both domestically and on the battlefield. Domestically, it has shown concern that its reliance on centralized electricity infrastructure leaves many of its critical units and buildings vulnerable to electricity outages, similar to those experienced by the civilian population. By reducing its dependence on centralized electricity generation, DoD will then be less exposed to power cuts and, in particular, sabotage of electricity generation. On the battlefield, emerging DPS applications enable the military to limit its reliance on diesel generation, which is vulnerable to supply disruptions (some of which can be fatal) and on unwieldy and inefficient battery packs, which are heavy and encumber the operation of U.S. ground forces.

Expert Forum

"I think one of the fundamental drivers for distributed generation and the smart grid principle is going to be around grid security and grid reliability, and, unfortunately, that's something that does not have a price today. . . . There is no stable market for grid security, and until there is a national-level realization of the need for actually introducing something like this, there's never really going to be mass adoption of these technologies, which do exist today."

—Pedram Mokrian, *Principal, Mayfield Fund*

The electric power supply security considerations discussed in this chapter lay bare the risks faced by both civilian and military end-users. Conference participants focused their discussion on how greater DPS deployment could contribute or be detrimental to the growing concern for grid cybersecurity. They also discussed how to think about valuing DPS ability to contribute to electricity system robustness and how that discussion shifts from a military perspective.

On measuring and valuing the effect of DPS on grid cybersecurity

On cybersecurity in SCADA systems and the Stuxnet worm: "No, there is no requirement to go tell a utility you shall do this. I think it's important to understand that the electric grid is run mainly by the private sector, owned by the private sector, and they're the ones who have to make the investments in that."

"Getting to the smart grid issue, technology is kind of a two-way sword here where we're going to get the benefits, but we've got to deploy it in a smart way. We want to be able to address those cybersecurity concerns and build it in up front, not build it on later."

—Hank Kenchington, *Deputy Assistant Secretary, Research and Development, Office of Electricity Delivery and Energy Reliability, U.S. Department of Energy*

On the business case for cybersecurity: "Generally what I learned in the counterintelligence world is that the name of the game is making it so expensive that it's prohibitive to your adversary. And so one way we can start to look at it is saying who is it that's trying to penetrate and how deep are their pockets, and starting to cost it that way rather than based on the consequences."

—Dennis McGinn (Vice Admiral, Retired), *President, American Council on Renewable Energy*

"I'm appreciating stepping through both the economic aspects and environmental aspects prior to the security aspects because taken alone, if we just focus on one, we come to the wrong conclusions."

—Bradley Schoener, *Energy Portfolio Manager, The MITRE Corporation*

With technology and infrastructure characteristics that differ from conventional energy systems, DPS affect the security of energy supply systems in which they operate. Conference speaker Bradley Schoener of the MITRE Corporation outlined how these characteristics specifically affect electricity system security in the face of cyber or physical attack. Benefits included:

- Microgrid islanding, which gives the ability to continue supplying electricity when a broader system is under cyber attack;
- The absence of single point of failure, which is desirable in itself and also makes for a more diffuse target if under attack;
- The ability to generate near load, which reduces potential attack target area as any weaknesses in transmission and distribution infrastructure become less relevant to the end-user;
- Added diversity in the fuel and generation mix, which makes the system less vulnerable to disruption of a single fuel;
- Added control over generation management by end-users.

Downside risks included:

- Uncertainty over the type and level of security practices implemented by numerous smaller-scale DPS developers and installers;
- More potential "points of entry" in a distributed infrastructure network, which expands the overall potential attack surface;
- The natural gas used to fuel DPS technologies such as microturbines may require storage tanks in urban

areas, which become potential targets due to their high flammability;

- Gas pipelines and distribution networks that fuel some distributed generation technologies may be less resilient to disruption than electricity grids, which can often be re-routed;

- Emerging DPS generation and storage technology supply chains are more likely to pass through foreign nations and this may introduce additional backdoor risks.

On the value of electricity system robustness to the U.S. military

On the security impact of implementing microgrids for U.S. bases running on civilian power: "When you have a Predator squadron that's operating out of Nevada that's controlling real life-and-death operations halfway around the world, you really want to have that power."

—Dennis McGinn (Vice Admiral, Retired),
President, American Council on Renewable Energy

"When I was visiting our CAOC, our Combined Air Operations Center, that coordinates the air strikes and air operations for all of our forces in Iraq and Afghanistan, they had a power outage and lights go out in the command center. Then they said, 'Don't worry, the generator will kick on.' And the generator did kick on and then a big cloud of smoke came out of it. Apparently a cat was playing near the generator and so we actually went down on power for a short period. Now fortunately, there was a third backup on top of it, but it shows you how small factors can have major, major consequences because you had thirty-six different strikes going on, all of which went blind for a couple of seconds when our cat met its fate."

—Peter Singer, *Senior Fellow and Director, 21st Century Defense Initiative, The Brookings Institution*

"They want to get as much resilience to the supply line as possible, as much range and endurance, they want to minimize the number of people who are exposed to risk moving things around the battle-field. Certainly we're interested in the fact that it saves money, too, but the primary reason is because it advances the mission."

"The closer you get to the fight, the more the returns may be non-monetary."

—Sharon Burke, *Assistant Secretary of Defense for Operational Energy Plans and Programs, U.S. Department of Defense*

Though needs and conditions vary across all potential DPS users, defense presents an exceptional case in its ability to directly capture the system value of robustness. Namely, the military on bases or in theater is often geographically wide-spread and isolated (from the scale of a base to an individual soldier), is a potential target for attack through the energy system, and may have time-inflexible demand. Defense applications also have high uptime and redundancy requirements for mission-critical operations, high technology usability requirements to match rapid end-user turnover or technology cycles, and special information security needs. Moreover, the armed forces operate daily in environments where loss of human life is a very real risk that may be mitigated by having the right equipment available in the right place.

So while civilian grid downtime can inflict substantial economic damage, the variety of stakeholders makes it difficult to distribute the costs needed for system investment to efficiently mitigate their combined risks. The military, in contrast, is a more coordinated single accounting entity and is therefore willing to invest in robustness and mission-specific performance. This has in some cases driven the military's interest in DPS ahead of civilian populations that might similarly benefit from such systems. One bonus to this has been the military's ability to nurture DPS technologies along declining cost curves until they become commercially viable under civilian economic calculations.

CHAPTER 4

CURRENT DPS POLICY LANDSCAPE

The preceding chapters described DPS technologies and their applications, summarized their evolving role in the U.S. power sector, and examined the costs and benefits of these systems. This chapter reviews the policy landscape with respect to DPS and serves to inform the feedback received from stakeholders in the power industry in Chapter 5.

At the federal, state, and local levels there are numerous policy mechanisms either designed specifically to promote DPS, or that more indirectly influence the deployment of these systems and resources. There are many excellent organizations and sources that assemble, monitor, update and, in some cases, rank the effectiveness of these policies and provide best practice guidelines for implementation.[1] It is not our intent to reproduce this information in its entirety, or to present exhaustive detail on each policy; rather it is the aim of this chapter to present a brief introduction to a selected group of policy tools that most directly affect DPS.[2]

For ease of analysis, we present these policies in three main categories:

- **Financial Incentives:** including tax exemptions and credits, loans, grants, and rebates;
- **Rules and Regulations:** such as renewable portfolio standards, interconnection standards, and net metering requirements; and
- **Strategies and Targets:** such as greenhouse gas reduction goals, and plans for the adoption of new technologies such as smart grid and plug-in electric vehicles.

This approach broadly follows the categorization of policies used by the Database of State Incentives for Renewables and Efficiency (DSIRE). Table 4.1 on page 93 summarizes current implementation as of late 2011; for additional details on policy design features and specific program examples at the state and federal level, please refer to DSIRE's website.

4.1 Federal Legislation

As outlined in Chapter 1, PURPA was the first major federal legislation that opened the way for greater deployment of distributed generation resources. PURPA created a wholesale market for non-utility, independent power projects and required utilities to connect these "qualifying facilities" (QFs) to their transmission grids. QFs produce electricity using alternative sources of power such as renewable fuels or cogeneration. Utilities are required to purchase power from QFs at the utility "avoided cost" of additional generation, with states left to develop methodologies for determining avoided cost.

In addition to PURPA, there have been several recent major pieces of federal legislation that have had a direct or indirect effect on the adoption of DPS.

- Energy Policy Act of 2005 (EPAct 2005)
- Energy Independence and Security Act of 2007 (EISA 2007)
- American Recovery and Reinvestment Act of 2009 (ARRA 2009)

Moreover, FERC has taken several actions influencing DPS-related issues, including interconnection standards, net metering, feed-in-tariffs, transmission, and storage.

In the following section, we highlight several illustrative federal provisions and rules dealing with DPS according to policy category.

Financial Incentives

There are many federal financial incentives for renewable energy and energy efficiency. In this section, we focus on three: tax incentives, loan guarantees, and accelerated depreciation.

Tax Incentives

Two major federal financial incentives having direct impact on DPS are the production tax credit (PTC) and the investment tax credit (ITC).

The PTC was initially enacted under the Energy Policy Act of 1992 and has been extended and amended many times over the years. It pays an inflation-adjusted tax credit for ten years, ranging from 1.1–2.2 cents per kWh depending on the technology.[3]

The ITC offers a tax credit equal to 30 percent of project costs for eligible technologies (solar, small wind) and 10 percent for others (geothermal, microturbines, and combined heat and power).[4]

Section 1603 of ARRA updated the PTC and the ITC:

- **PTC:** Facilities eligible for the PTC can elect to choose the 30 percent ITC or to receive a cash grant from the U.S. Treasury Department covering up to 30 percent of the project cost (under a new program referred to as a 1603 grant).
- **ITC:** Facilities eligible for the ITC can choose to receive a 1603 cash grant covering up to 30 percent of the project cost.

Federal Loan Guarantee Program

EPAct 2005 authorized support for innovative clean energy technologies that are typically unable to obtain conventional private financing due to high technology risks. These technologies must also avoid, reduce, or sequester air pollutants or greenhouse gases.[5] The act authorized loan guarantees for certain renewable energy systems (including solar, wind, and biomass), electric power transmission systems, and leading edge biofuels projects.[6] By guaranteeing loans and agreeing to repay a borrower's debt obligation in the event of a default for eligible clean energy projects, the program provides a more secure environment for investors. The program also provides direct loans to manufacturers of advanced-technology vehicles. In this manner, the mission is "to accelerate the domestic commercial deployment of innovative and advanced clean energy technologies at a scale sufficient to contribute meaningfully to the achievement of our national clean energy objectives."[7] Thus far, the DOE's Loans Programs Office has guaranteed $26.67 billion.[8]

Modified Accelerated Cost-Recovery System

MACRS incentivizes the use of renewable energy by allowing depreciation of eligible renewable generation assets.[9] The terms of cost recovery differ according to the technology involved: solar electric and solar thermal, fuel cells, microturbines, geothermal electric, wind installations under 100 kW, and combined heat and power applications are each considered "five-year property," allowing them to be depreciated over five years. Recent amendments to the program introduced a first-year "bonus" depreciation of 50 percent for eligible renewable energy systems purchased and installed.[10]

Rules and Regulations

Federal rules and regulations also affect DPS deployment, especially in the areas of net metering and interconnection and FERC has issued several decisions dealing with jurisdictional issues related to DPS development.

Net Metering and Interconnection

Two provisions of EPAct 2005 were directly beneficial for the adoption of distributed power systems, through the requirements for utilities to provide net metering and interconnection service.[11]

Before the passage of EPAct 2005, utilities determined the standards and technical requirements for the interconnection of

> ### Net Metering and Interconnection Standards
>
> **Net Metering:** For electric customers who generate their own electricity, net metering allows for the flow of electricity both to and from the customer—typically through a single, bi-directional meter. When a customer's generation exceeds the customer's use, electricity from the customer flows back to the grid, offsetting electricity consumed by the customer at a different time during the same billing cycle.
>
> **Interconnection Standards:** These specify the technical and procedural process by which a customer connects an electricity-generating unit to the grid, including the technical and contractual terms that system owners and utilities must abide by.
>
> *Source:* www.dsireusa.org

distributed resources. However, in a 2000 study by the National Renewable Energy Laboratory of sixty-five distributed power case studies, only seven reported no major utility related barriers to interconnection. A majority of respondents noted that "utilities' policies or practices constituted unnecessary barriers to interconnection."[12] With distributed power systems accounting for upward of 15 percent of electricity generation capacity in some regions of the country, there was growing concern around the reliability implications of further interconnections. These provisions of EPAct 2005 were designed to promote more widespread adoption of net metering and interconnection rates.

In November 2005, FERC required all public utilities involved in interstate commerce to implement standard interconnection procedures for small generators (those under 20 MW).[13] Under the order, small generators are required to adhere to FERC's Small Generator Interconnection Procedures for technical issues and the Small Generator Interconnection

Agreement for contractual issues. It also required that all utilities under its jurisdiction implement open access transmission tariffs (OATTs). According to FERC, the regulation was designed to equalize interconnection treatment for generators both independent of and affiliated with transmission providers. The order was designed to "reduce interconnection time and costs [. . .], preserve reliability, increase energy supply where needed, lower wholesale prices for customers by increasing the number and types of new generation that will compete in the wholesale electricity market, facilitate development of non-polluting alternative energy sources, and help remedy undue discrimination."[14] However, the interconnection standards apply only to utilities subject to FERC's jurisdiction; as most small generators are at the distribution level, the policy has little applicability to the majority of distributed power systems.

FERC Jurisdiction

Over the last decade, FERC has made several rulings having an impact on DPS, especially small-scale facilities and installations.

In March 2001, FERC stated that "we find . . . that no sale occurs when an individual homeowner or farmer (or similar entity such as a business) installs generation and accounts for its dealings with the utility through the practice of netting."[15] In effect, this ruling seemed to define that the process of net metering does not constitute a sale of electricity from a customer-sited facility, but rather a crediting arrangement. However, FERC has left open the possibility that where a sale occurs, it could constitute a wholesale transaction and thus fall within its jurisdiction.[16]

EPAct 2005 ended the mandatory purchase requirements stipulated in PURPA for those QFs with access to wholesale markets, i.e. the exemption applied to utilities operating only in "sufficiently competitive markets for the QF to sell its power."[17] Following passage of the EPAct 2005, FERC issued a generic rule removing the purchase obligation for utilities connecting to four independent system operators—Midwest Independent System Operator, PJM Interconnection, ISO-New England, and the New York Independent System Operator[18]—and gave utilities in other regions the opportunity to file applications for relief from the obligation. Notably, the exemption does not apply to QFs with a net capacity of less than 20 MW; i.e., utilities still have the obligation to purchase from facilities with a capacity up to 20 MW.

More recent FERC actions affecting DPS include:

- Exempting QFs under 1 MW from requirements to self-certify or request QF certification from FERC,[19] and
- Clarifying that avoided costs can be calculated taking into consideration specific state requirements for renewable technologies and that different avoided costs rates can be used for various renewable technologies.[20]

In sum, with regard to federal jurisdiction over DPS projects, if no power is sold back to the grid or if a third-party owner of on-site generation sells power only to the host, there is no transaction subject to federal jurisdiction.[21] Furthermore:

"If the on-site facility is interconnected to the local distribution grid or to an independent system operator or local or regional wholesale market, potentially the transaction could be subject to federal regulation under the Federal Power Act and FERC rules, but so long as the on-site generation qualifies as a QF, or is a small power generating facility, no federal regulation applies."[22]

FERC has also initiated a process to examine approaches for quantifying the benefits of storage, specifically seeking comment on "how to remove potential barriers to the expanded use of electric storage technologies . . . [since] current procedures do not specifically provide for the accounting of costs related to new energy storage resources and operations, nor do they clearly indicate how best to classify storage technologies that can provide a range of services to the grid."[23]

Strategies and Targets

The federal government has taken a strong lead in promoting several key broad strategies and plans that have an impact on DPS, especially regarding the promotion of the smart grid, electric vehicles, and storage.

Smart Grid

The U.S. DOE defines the smart grid as "a class of technology people are using to bring utility electricity delivery systems into the twenty-first century, using computer-based remote control and automation."[24] Both EISA 2007 and ARRA 2009 directly supported the smart grid.

Energy Independence and Security Act 2007

EISA 2007 contains several provisions aimed at increasing the penetration of distributed resources, explicitly acknowledging "distributed resources and generation, including renewable resources" as a constituent part of the smart grid.[25]

EISA 2007 designated the National Institute for Science and Technology (NIST) as the organization to coordinate a framework and roadmap for smart grid interoperability standards and protocols. In January 2010 NIST released its *Framework and Roadmap for Smart Grid Interoperability Standards*, which prioritized six "key functionalities" of the smart grid in which the timely creation of standards were most needed. Two of these areas, "demand response and consumer energy efficiency" and "energy storage" have direct applicability to distributed resources. Through its Interoperability Framework Process, NIST devises Priority Action Plans, which define challenges, establish objectives, and seek to identify the standards necessary to meet them. NIST recognizes the importance of energy storage in combination with distributed energy resources as a "key priority . . . in the interoperability standards development process."[26]

American Recovery and Reinvestment Act 2009

DPS applications were also given a boost by ARRA's $4.5 billion allocation for the smart grid. The bill explicitly states that one of the measures of the economic and environmental impact of smart grid investments and demonstrations is "the percentage increase of total load served [measured in MW] by smart-grid-enabled distributed energy resources, renewable energy systems, and energy storage devices." The inclusion of "distributed generation" and "load served by microgrids" in the DOE's formal "build metrics" for the grid shows that advancing the cause of DPS is a leading objective of the ARRA 2009 legislation.

Electric Vehicles

ARRA allowed buyers of new qualified plug-in cars sold after Dec. 31, 2009 to receive a tax credit between $2,500 and $7,500 according to the car's battery capacity.[27] The latter condition is relevant to DPS as it serves to incentivize batteries with larger storage capacities, which are likely to provide more options for distributed vehicle-to-grid storage.

Storage

EISA 2007 allocates funding to a research, development, and demonstration program, an Energy Storage Advisory Council, and four energy storage research centers.[28] In total, the act allocates nearly $3 billion to storage-related development. Technologies and applications explicitly covered include a range of transmission and grid-related applications likely to advance the development of distributed storage and, in turn, strengthen the case for distributed generation sources, including:

- Islanding, defined as "a distributed generator or energy storage device continuing to power a location in the absence of electric power from the primary source," and
- Microgrid, defined as "an integrated energy system consisting of interconnected loads and distributed energy resources (including generators and energy storage devices), which as an integrated system can operate in parallel with the utility grid or in an intentional islanding mode."

4.2 State-Level Legislation

Across the fifty states and the District of Columbia there are numerous policies to promote DPS specifically, and renewable energy and energy efficiency generally. As noted at the beginning of this chapter, there are many excellent sources describing these policy tools, including advantages and disadvantages and best practices in design. For the purposes of this section, we focus on specific policy tools utilized by the states with the most influence on DPS.[29]

Financial Incentives

Tax Incentives

One of the most common financial mechanisms at the state level is the encouragement of distributed generation through tax incentives. These can be tax exemptions or tax credits.

Tax exemptions are at the personal level through income tax exemptions or property tax exemptions for commercial, industrial, or residential projects. Tax exemptions are an effective, albeit potentially expensive, way for states to incentivize the adoption of distributed power systems. Exemptions fall into two broad categories: the exemption of taxes that would otherwise be paid on the purchase and installation of the systems themselves, and the partial exemption of taxes on properties whose value is increased by the addition of distributed power systems. Both types are very common, although the details of such policies vary from state to state with regard to the kind of qualifying facility.

Tax credits are another means of incentivizing distributed power systems, giving owners a defined reduction in tax liability.

An ITC represents a share of the system cost while a PTC is based on measured system output.

Source: Clean Energy States Alliance

They fall into one of two main categories: PTCs and ITCs. Such tax credits allow renewable energy system owners to lower the cost of the energy system through a credit on either personal or corporate state income taxes.[30] Tax credits often have caps on the amount of funding available, with commercial systems having higher caps than residential systems. It is possible for a project to qualify for both state and federal tax credits.

Grants and Loans

Grants are one type of financial support usually given to "larger, less standard projects where the degree of required project support and the expected energy output of the project can vary considerably."[31] They are provided to projects at various stages of development, from feasibility to construction and can be established based on specific criteria and strategic program objectives so that grant managers can be more discerning in choosing projects.[32]

Loans have been used for renewable energy and energy efficiency programs to "reduce upfront cost barriers of renewable energy systems and to improve upon the standard credit and lending terms that may be available for these systems from private lenders."[33]

Rebates

A whole array of state rebates is used to promote the installation and use of DPS. Rebates are "lump-sum payments that cover a portion of a renewable energy project's capital cost and are normally paid to the project owner upon project installation."[34] They are also usually capped at a dollar amount or at a percentage of total system costs and must meet various eligibility requirements.[35]

Feed-In-Tariffs

A feed-in tariff is a "standard offering from a utility for a fixed-price contract for electricity produced from a renewable energy generator for a specified term length."[36] Within the United States, FITs are currently established in five states, implemented by four cities and one major utility in another state, and being proposed and considered in several other states.[37]

Under the terms of a FIT, certain utilities are obligated to buy electricity from renewable electricity system owners at long-term fixed rates established by regulatory entities and such offerings can be limited to certain technologies, system size, or project location.[38] FITs act to guarantee a certain price, a long-term revenue stream, and grid interconnection so that financial risks are reduced for investments in certain technologies that policymakers and regulators may want to promote for environmental or other reasons. FITs are usually implemented when the preferred resource is unable to compete on a cost basis or has other significant barriers to market penetration. They are designed to develop a market for certain types of energy technologies, such as renewable or other DPS, so that those technologies can compete without support after the terms of the contract.

The advantages of a FIT include the fact that it is a performance-based incentive that awards actual generated energy instead of only installed capacity, it facilitates financing and investment that would otherwise be difficult by ensuring predictability and stability in the market, and it allows for a competitive rate of return on investment if properly established.[39]

FITs can be either cost- or value-based. One major drawback of cost-based FITs is the increased cost to consumers and ratepayers that result from their price usually being set above the

TABLE 4.1 SELECTED DPS-RELATED POLICIES

	Financial Incentives						Rules & Regulations			
	Tax Incentives		Rebates	Grants	Loans	Feed-In Tariffs	RPS	Net Metering	Inter-Connection Standards	Output-Based Emissions
	Corporate	Personal								
Federal	√	√		√	√				√	
States										
Alabama		√	Local	√	√					
Alaska				√	√			√	√	
Arizona	√	√	Local		Local		√(SC)	√	Local	
Arkansas			Local		√			√	√	√
California			√		√	√	√	√	√	√
Colorado			Local	Local	√		√(SC)	√	√	
Connecticut			√	√	√		√(C)	√	√	√
Delaware			√		√		√(S)	√	√	√
Florida			Local		√	Local	Local	√	√	
Georgia	√	√	Local	Local	√			√	√	
Hawaii	√	√	√		√	√	√(C)	√	√	
Idaho		√	Local	Local	√			Local		
Illinois			√	√	√		√(SC)	√	√	√
Indiana		√	Local		Local		√	√	√	√
Iowa	√	√	Local		√		√(C)	√	√	
Kansas	√	√	Local		√		√	√	√	
Kentucky	√	√	√		√			√	√	
Louisiana	√	√	√		√			√	√	
Maine			√	√	√	√	√(C)	√	√	√
Maryland	√	√	√		√		√(S)	√	√	
Massachusetts	√	√	√	√	√		√(SC)	√	√	
Michigan			Local	√	√	Local	√(C)	√	√	
Minnesota			√	√	√		√(C)	√	√	
Mississippi			Local		√					
Missouri	√		Local		√		√(SC)	√	√	√
Montana	√	√	Local	Local	√		√	√	√	
Nebraska	√	√	Local		√			√	√	
Nevada			√		√		√(SC)	√	√	
New Hampshire			√	√	√		√(SC)	√	√	√
New Jersey			√		√		√(SC)	√	√	√
New Mexico	√	√	Local		√		√(SC)	√	√	
New York	√	√	√	√	√		√(SC)	√	√	√
North Carolina	√	√	Local		√		√(SC)	√	√	
North Dakota	√	√	Local		√		√(C)	√		
Ohio			Local		√		√(SC)	√	√	√
Oklahoma	√		Local		√		√(C)	√		
Oregon	√	√	√	√	√	√	√(SC)	√	√	√
Pennsylvania			√	√	√		√(SC)	√	√	
Rhode Island	√	√		√	√		√(C)	√	√	
South Carolina	√	√	Local		√			Local	√	
South Dakota			Local		√		√(C)		√	
Tennessee			Local	√	√					
Texas	√		Local	√	√	Local	√(C)	Local	√	√
Utah	√	√	√				√(C)	√	√	
Vermont	√		√	Local	√	√	√(C)	√	√	

TABLE 4.1 SELECTED DPS-RELATED POLICIES *(CONTINUED)*

	Financial Incentives						Rules & Regulations			
	Tax Incentives		Rebates	Grants	Loans	Feed-In Tariffs	RPS	Net Metering	Inter-Connection Standards	Output-Based Emissions
	Corporate	Personal								
Virginia			√		√		√	√	√	
Washington			Local	Local	Local		√(C)	√	√	√
West Virginia	√	√	Local				√	√	√	
Wisconsin	√	√	√		√	Local	√	√	√	√
Wyoming			Local		√			√	√	
District of Col.			√		√		√(S)	√	√	

Sources and Notes for Table: All data from the DSIRE website,[40] except where otherwise noted.

A check mark indicates that the policy exists at the state-level (but may also exist at the utility and local levels); "Local" indicates the policy does not exist at the state-level but does exist at the utility and/or local levels; for RPS, S indicates Solar/DG set-aside within an RPS; C indicates CHP set-aside within some type of portfolio standard.

CHP data under Renewable Portfolio Standards and output-based emissions data are from the American Council for an Energy-Efficient Economy (ACEEE).[41] CHP can be eligible under different types of state policies, including Renewable Portfolio Standards, Alternative Energy Portfolio Standards, and/or Energy Efficiency Portfolio Standards.

Feed-In Tariffs from the National Association of Regulatory Utility Commissioners.[42]

market price in order to encourage investment. "Balancing the urgency of renewable energy development with limiting unnecessary costs [to ratepayers] to ensure development will be an important consideration for policymakers interested in renewable energy" and distributed power systems.[43] However, there may be beneficial impacts in the local economy such as job creation.

In addition, states are potentially limited in setting requirements for utilities to pay for electricity at a certain cost since the Federal Power Act and PURPA give the federal government jurisdiction over wholesale power rates.[44] However, as previously noted, recent rulings by FERC have tried to clarify such uncertainties.[45]

Rules and Regulations

Renewable Portfolio Standards

Renewable Portfolio Standards (RPS) are the primary renewable energy policy mechanism used in the United States: twenty-nine states and Washington, DC, have an RPS, while eight states have established non-binding renewable portfolio goals. Lawrence Berkeley National Laboratory indicates that RPS in place applied to 47 percent of U.S. load in 2010, which will rise to 56 percent when fully implemented. Moreover, 23 GW of non-hydro renewable capacity (mostly wind) was added in the period from 1998 to 2009 in states with active or impending RPS compliance obligations.[46]

RPS are designed to stimulate the least-cost procurement of renewable energy and thus tend to disadvantage smaller DPS. To address this, some states are developing carve-outs, or separate targets within overall requirements, for particular technologies,

---

Renewable Portfolio Standards require utilities to use renewable energy or renewable energy credits (RECs) to account for a certain percentage of their retail electricity sales — or a certain amount of generating capacity — according to a specified schedule.

Source: www.dsireusa.org

such as solar, distributed generation, or CHP (see Table 4.2). Most of the DPS-related carve outs are targeted to solar PV, while only four states—Arizona, Colorado, New Mexico, and New York—have specific targets for non-PV DG (Washington offers double credit for DG projects).[47]

TABLE 4.2 SUMMARY OF STATE RPS WITH SOLAR/DG SET-ASIDES AND MULTIPLIERS

State	Overall RPS Requirements	Solar or DG Requirement
Arizona	15% by 2025	4.5% DG by 2025
Colorado	30% by 2020 for IOUs; 10% by 2020 for coops and large munis	3% DG by 2020; 1.5 % customer sited x 2020
D.C.	20% by 2020	2.5% solar by 2023
Delaware	25% by 2026	3.5 % PV by 2026; 3x multiplier for PV
Illinois	25% by 2025	1.5% solar PV by 2025
Maryland	20% by 2022	2% solar electric by 2022
Massachusetts	22.1% by 2020; (new RE by 15% by 2020 and +1% per year after)	400 MW PV by 2020
Michigan	10% & 1,100 MW by 2015	3x multiplier for solar-electric
Missouri	15% by 2021	0.3% solar-electric by 2021
Nevada	25% by 2025	1.5% solar by 2025; 2.4–2.45x multiplier for PV
New Hampshire	23.8% by 2025	0.3% solar-electric by 2014
New Jersey	20.38% RE by 2021	5,316 GWh solar electric by 2026
New Mexico	20% by 2020 for IOUs and 10% by 2020 for coops	4% solar-electric by 2020; 0.6% DG by 2020
New York	29% by 2015	0.4788% customer-sited DG by 2015
North Carolina	12.5% by 2021 for IOUs and 10% by 2018 for coops and munis	0.2% solar by 2018
Ohio	25% by 2025	0.5% solar electric by 2025
Oregon	25% by 2025 for large utilities and 5–10% by 2025 for smaller utilities	20MW solar PV by 2020; 2x multiplier PV
Pennsylvania	18% by 2021	0.5% solar PV by 2021
Texas	5,880 MW by 2015	2x multiplier for all non-wind projects (500 MW non-wind goal)
Utah	20% by 2025	2.4x multiplier for solar-electric
Washington	15% by 2020	Double credit for DG
West Virginia	25% by 2025	Various multipliers

Source: DSIRE Summary Maps (http://dsireusa.org/summarymaps /index.cfm?ee=1&RE=1).

Net Metering

Since EPAct 2005 obligated state utility commissions and non-regulated utilities to consider net metering, more net metering policies have been established. Currently, forty-three states and Washington, DC, have net metering policies in place, and three states have utility voluntary programs only. The number of net-metered systems has increased substantially since 2002 (see Figure 4.1).

Several groups, including the Interstate Renewable Energy Council (IREC), the Network for New Energy Choices (NNEC) and the American Council for an Energy-Efficient Economy

FIGURE 4.1 GROWING NUMBER OF NET-METERED SYSTEMS

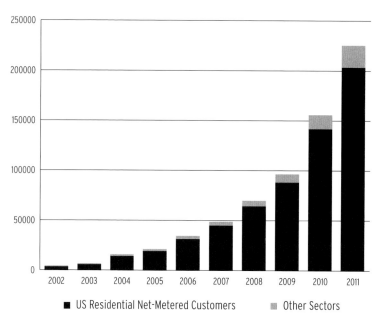

Source: EIA Form 861 Database as shown in IREC (2009) "Connecting to the Grid," p. 13.

(ACEEE) track and assess state net metering policies, evaluating their effectiveness and developing best practice guidelines. IREC has also developed—and continues to modify and update—its own net-metering model rules.[48] IREC's publication "Connecting to the Grid" provides a comprehensive summary of technical and policy considerations surrounding these design aspects.[49]

Interconnection Standards

In the early 2000s, the lack of interconnection standards was increasingly identified as providing a significant barrier to greater deployment of DPS.[50] In 2003, IEEE finalized standard 1547 (Standard for Interconnecting Distributed Resources with Electric Power Systems) specifying the basic technical requirements for interconnection. EPAct 2005 obligated state utility commissions and non-regulated utilities to consider adopting interconnection procedures using IEEE 1547. By 2006, several model rules and procedures for connecting distributed generation systems were developed. The most important of these were:[51]

- California Rule 21
- FERC Small Generator Interconnection Procedures
- Mid-Atlantic Demand Resource Initiative Procedures (MADRI Procedures)
- IREC Model Interconnection Procedures (IREC Procedures)
- NARUC Small Generation Resource Interconnection Procedures

Many states have since instituted standard interconnection rules: currently, forty-three states and Washington, DC, have an interconnection policy in place.

Rate Mechanisms and Issues

A utility with full decoupling in place will generally recover any reduction in electricity sales from net metering. Decoupling is a mechanism that "decouples" a utility's kWh sales from its revenue thereby allowing a utility to recover its fixed costs even when its electricity sales are lower than expected. Decoupling is typically used to align utility incentives so that utilities have no disincentive for promoting energy efficiency which decreases sales; however, this regulatory mechanism also works in the context of net metering and distributed power generation. Without decoupling, a utility that experiences a decrease in sales (below the expected sales forecast) would not recover enough revenue to cover its fixed costs. However, in some states, utilities have partial decoupling or a lost revenue adjustment mechanism related solely to energy efficiency. In these instances, a utility would not recover reduced sales due to net metering unless specific language allowed this type of recovery. As of June, 2011, in the United States, about thirteen states have decoupling mechanisms in place with another nine pending, and nine states have lost-revenue recovery mechanisms in place with two pending; the specifics of these mechanisms vary from state to state.[52] The number of states with a decoupling or lost-revenue recovery mechanism in place has grown significantly over the past few years and it is expected that more states will adopt such mechanisms.

A general issue related to almost all retail electric sales is the fact that retail electricity rates, for the most part, do not take into account the varying cost of generating electricity by time of day, day of the week, season of the year, or other grid conditions. Most, but not all, residential and small commercial customers pay a fixed rate for electricity consumption that does not vary dynamically. This topic has been debated for several decades and with the rollout of smart meters to mass market customers, the opportunity to provide dynamic rates (i.e., rates that are related to the price of wholesale power) has now moved closer to the forefront of the policy debate. Several state PUCs are discussing this issue with plans to provide rate options to small retail customers down the road. These rates can vary from fixed time of day rates to critical peak pricing and real-time rates. Technically speaking, the most effective rates are those that are dispatchable (time of day rates are not dispatchable) and therefore related to the wholesale price of electricity.

This issue affects DPS in that a customer supplying power to the grid at a peak hour of the day when the wholesale price of electricity is high should receive a different price for that power than if the same power is supplied at 10:00 p.m. However, at this time, most states have chosen to adopt net metering mechanisms which currently, by running the meter backwards, result in a customer receiving the retail rate for power produced. In most instances, the customer does not get paid for producing excess power but this is changing. As these policies develop and evolve, it makes sense for excess power produced to be purchased at the wholesale rate (essentially a dynamic real-time rate is equivalent to the wholesale price of power). However, the price of electricity is not the only cost when supplying power to the grid; fees related to the grid, such as distribution system costs, will also need to be considered and included.

Output-Based Emissions

Electricity generation has traditionally been subject to input-based emissions regulations—limiting the amount of emissions produced per unit of input fuel (e.g., pounds of sulfur dioxide per million Btu of coal). However, this does not recognize the efficiency of the process in converting the fuel input into a useful output and so depends upon pollution control devices to reduce emissions without directly incentivizing plant efficiency.

The regulation of output-based emissions seeks to encourage efficiency and renewable energy while also controlling air pollution. Output-based emissions regulation "levels the playing field by establishing performance criteria and allowing efficiency and renewable energy to compete on equal footing with other methods of reducing emissions."[53] Such regulations define "emissions limits based on the amount of pollution produced per unit of useful output (e.g., pounds of sulfur dioxide per megawatt-hour of electricity)."[54] More specifically, output-based regulations include both output-based emission standards and output-based allocations of emission allowances within a cap-and-trade program.[55] In short, output-based emissions regulation decreases emissions in the energy generation process by recognizing the efficiency of plants—for example, combined heat and power (CHP). Moreover, output-based emissions allow comparisons between different technologies by using a common unit for their emissions rather than more varied units of measuring input fuels. Without using output-based regulations, the thermal energy outputs of CHP will not be able to be included in emission calculations.

In 2003, the Regulatory Assistance Project (RAP) released a national, model emission rule for distributed generation systems.[56] RAP noted that in the long-run, "the industry, the electric system, and the environment will be better served by a set of like rules across states and regions" rather than "a hodgepodge of inconsistent and even incompatible rules" with each region setting its own standards and requirements.[57] Many different technologies and fuel types are included in DPS and these different types allow for different emissions characteristics. Therefore, RAP attempted to formulate a rule that is "intended to regulate the emissions of a class of generators that are not covered, or not covered consistently, under existing state or federal regulations."[58] The model rule regulates five air pollutants: nitrogen oxides, particulate matter, carbon monoxide, sulfur dioxide, and carbon dioxide. Therefore, output-based emissions regulation serves not only to encourage DPS, but also to ensure that air quality is enhanced regardless of the fuel type and generation source. The proposed RAP Model Rule for output-based emissions calculates credits for thermal output avoided through the use of CHP systems.

Currently, seventeen states have some sort of output-based emissions regulation. There are several forms in which output-based emissions regulations can occur: conventional emission limits (such as in California or Texas), small distributed generation policy (such as in Connecticut), allowance trading (such as in Massachusetts) or allowance set-asides (such as in Indiana), and emissions performance standards (such as in California, Oregon, and Washington).[59]

Strategies and Targets

Climate Action Plans

Climate Action Plans are developed by states to reduce their contribution to climate change. The effectiveness of Climate Action Plans is dependent upon the clarity of stated policies, the types of incentives, and the existence of emissions reduction targets.

Climate Action Plans are important for distributed power systems because they formulate the overall direction for climate policy in the state, providing investors and customers with a

Climate Action Plans identify cost-effective opportunities to reduce GHG emissions that are relevant to the state.

GHG Emissions Targets represent the commitment by a state to reduce its GHG emissions by a certain level within a specific time-frame.

Source: Pew Center on Global Climate Change

stable and transparent decision-making environment. The recommendations of Climate Action Plans often include many of the other incentives and policies discussed in this report. Currently, thirty-six states have completed Climate Action Plans, with an additional two states in the process of doing so.

GHG Emissions Targets

A greenhouse gas (GHG) emissions target is often included within Climate Action Plans and is generally considered a key policy component for reducing the effects of climate change, as well as a mechanism to support renewable DPS. According to the Pew Center, twenty-three states have already implemented GHG emissions targets. These states generally have targets for reducing emissions to levels of a predetermined past year by a certain deadline year in the future.

PHEV Policy

PHEVs have gained more attention in recent years and represent a potential key component of DPS as storage devices connected to the grid. Plug-in hybrid electric vehicles are promoted principally through three types of policy mechanisms: fleet vehicle acquisition requirements, preferred roadway and parking access, and financial incentives. The first category involves mandates for certain fleets in the state to acquire PHEVs. The second type of policy provides access to certain lanes and parking areas to PHEVs. Financial incentives include credits, rebates, grants, and other approaches to promote PHEVs. There are currently thirty-five states that have some sort of PHEV policy involving a combination of these policies.[60]

Smart Grid Policy

The drivers for state smart grid policies vary but generally include concerns about climate change and the desire to add renewable capacity, the deferral of costly new power plants or transmission lines, the need for higher levels of efficiency and demand response, support for mass deployment of electric vehicles, and ensuring reliability.[61] The Institute for Electric Efficiency (IEE) notes that 27 million smart meters have been installed in the United States as of September 2011 and estimates that by 2015 approximately 65 million will be deployed, representing 54 percent of U.S. households.[62] IEE also calculates that 20 states and the District of Columbia have deployed smart meters to more than 50 percent of end-users.[63] In addition, about twelve states have instituted some regulatory action for smart grid cost recovery, including adjustable tariff riders, surcharges, and rate base recovery.[64]

4.3 Local Rules

Different states, counties, and municipalities have their own regulations and permitting rules for the construction and installation of distributed power systems, involving noise ordinance, land-use restrictions, and other siting and zoning issues. State and local zoning boards, state and local environmental protection agencies, as well as the Federal Bureau of Land Management may all be involved to different degrees. In some regions, permitting jurisdiction is subject to both local and state requirements. This has significant impact on cost-benefit analysis for small-scale distributed power systems because it requires installers to not only consider the physical characteristics of potential sites for DPS but also the perceptions of the community, the local government, and the state government toward DPS. In short, local rules can add significant costs to projects, especially for smaller companies or residential customers who do not have the resources or awareness to navigate the process.

Several states are trying to address these local issues. Recently Colorado passed HB 1199, the Fair Permit Act, which will "limit solar permit and related fees to a local government's actual costs in issuing the permit, not to exceed $500 for residential installation or $1,000 for a commercial system. The bill also closed loopholes and improves transparency in the permit process."[65] In addition, the Vote Solar Initiative has developed best-practice guidelines addressing fees and streamlining a variety of administrative requirements.[66]

4.4 Other Recent Policy Initiatives

There are several other specific policy mechanisms that are gaining traction among policymakers. Here we highlight several of the more relevant for renewable energy and DPS.

Reverse Auction Mechanism

In December 2010, the California Public Utilities Commission (CPUC) approved a Reverse Auction Mechanism (RAM) to allow renewable energy developers to bid on small-scale projects that would generate up to 1000 MW in California, to be shared among Pacific Gas & Electric, Southern California Edison, and San Diego Gas & Electric.[67] The market is for renewable electricity projects with a generation capacity of up to 20 MW. Such small-scale plants are preferred because they can be constructed relatively quickly and connected to the grid without significant transmission upgrades.

According to the new regulation, developers will be required to calculate the cost of the projects in order to offer bids. Those bids need to be both high enough to generate profits and also low enough to be competitive. The expectation is that such an approach will avoid the concerns associated with cost-based feed-in tariffs. As previously noted, a major challenge with FITs is the difficulty of setting appropriate prices and determining the impact on ratepayers. In creating the RAM, the CPUC noted that: "Providing a clear and steady long-term investment signal rather than providing a pre-determined price can create a competitive market."[68]

Energy Improvement Districts

Energy Improvement Districts (EID)—also referred to as Neighborhood Energy Partnerships and Energy Independence Districts—refer to a concept in which multiple participants are allowed to form a separate entity to finance and administer their own energy resources within a defined geographic area. This builds on the business improvement districts developed several decades ago to address a variety of local issues and services, such as sanitation. The EID allows participants to share costs, benefits, and administrative requirements in financing and implementing energy projects. EIDs are usually accorded legal status and permitted to issue bonds, as well, to install wires.

Connecticut established legislation in 2007 creating EIDs and identified customer-side distributed resources, grid-side distributed resources, and combined heat and power systems as "energy improvement district distributed resources."[69]

One key issue related to EIDs is that of "private wires." This refers to the ability of an owner of an on-site generation facility to serve adjacent customers through privately-owned distribution lines, i.e., not using the local utility's network.[70] Typically, private wires have not been permitted owing to concerns over duplication of service, reliability, and safety and the legal constraint that local electric utilities are the sole entity authorized to install wires and provide electricity. However, a few jurisdictions are beginning to loosen these restrictions. For example, the Public Service Commission in New York ruled in 2007 that a cogeneration facility could install distribution wires and a pipeline across a public way to provide electricity and heat to off-site customers.[71]

Virtual Net Metering

Virtual net metering (VNM) allows customers with multiple non-contiguous accounts to offset consumption at multiple locations. A VNM pilot program in California seeks to enable multi-tenant buildings to benefit from net metering across multiple units. California's AB 2466 of 2008 allows local governments to distribute bill credits from a renewable energy system across more than one meter. Originally, VNM was available only to customers participating in the Multifamily Affordable Solar Housing program, but was extended to all multi-tenant properties and all distributed generation technologies.[72]

Multi-tenant buildings have historically faced problems in DPS installation because of the difficulty of connecting the system to multiple loads while ensuring the equitable distribution of the power produced. Installing multiple DPS would also be cost-prohibitive. By allowing DPS to be connected to a single delivery point, the produced energy is fed back onto the grid instead of directly to the tenants. The utility then "allocates kilowatt hours from the energy produced by the [distributed] generating system to both the building owners' and tenants' individual utility accounts, based on a pre-arranged allocation agreement."[73]

Community Choice Aggregators

The Community Choice Aggregators (CCA) program, established in California by AB 117, allows service areas to purchase and/or generate electricity for themselves while the utilities deliver the electricity through their transmission and distribution systems.[74] It allows California cities to supply their own electricity to customers within a limited area,[75] and local regions can aggregate the electric loads of all residents and businesses in the area in order to facilitate the purchase and sale of electrical energy. Individuals are able to opt-out of the program.[76] The program provides communities with the option to increase their renewable fuel sources if they so desire and to choose the fuel mix for their own energy use. Besides in California, CCAs also exist in Ohio, Massachusetts, and Rhode Island.[77]

Master Limited Partnerships for Renewable Energy Projects

A Master Limited Partnership (MLP) is a type of business structure "that is taxed as a partnership, but whose ownership interests are traded on financial markets like corporate stock."[78] The difference is that, for tax purposes, partnerships are "generally subject to one layer of taxation in contrast to publicly-traded . . .

corporations, which are subject to two layers of taxation."[79] As a result, combining benefits of two types of business structures means that MLPs can secure capital at lower costs because they have access both to more capital and favorable tax treatment.[80] There is rising interest in using MLPs as mechanism to provide additional financing for renewable energy projects.[81] However, legislation generally has excluded renewable energy entities from access to MLP status.

4.5 Summary Observations

There is a wide variety of policy mechanisms that have an impact on DPS—both directly and indirectly—developed and implemented by entities at the federal, state, and local levels. These tools can be more market-based to leverage and promote private sector activity and interest, or rely on more direct government involvement in the market. They can be designed to influence quantity or price. They can be technology neutral, or designed to support a specific technology. Currently the states have the most robust role. The leading policies in support of DPS and renewable energy generally are RPS, net metering, interconnection standards, and selected financial incentives, principally tax credits and exemptions, rebates, loans, and grants.

Expert Forum

"Regulatory capture is the rule, not the exception. Nevertheless, it's so that regulations can be drawn in such a way that they encourage activity, rather than suppress it."

—George P. Shultz, *Thomas W. and Susan B. Ford Distinguished Fellow, The Hoover Institution*

"We would rather focus on an outcomes-based approach or an attributes-based approach as opposed to trying to say solar at the expense of microturbines or vice versa."

—Andrew Karsner, *Executive Chairman, Manifest Energy*

As described in this study, current policies towards DPS are diverse and represent varying goals and regulatory approaches. Conference participants questioned the interests of various regulatory bodies toward broader DPS deployment and discussed the potential for policy to become a barrier to DPS as attitudes and technologies evolve. Issues such as rate design in the face of DPS uptake are already exposing the difficulty in trying to regulate around rapid innovation in technology and business models while still using mechanisms designed for an increasingly anachronistic electricity system paradigm.

On diversity in state-level regulation

"So if there ever was a hodgepodge-quilt, state laboratory for something it would be this. This is the furthest thing from uniform national policy that we probably have in the energy domain to talk about."

—Andrew Karsner, *Executive Chairman, Manifest Energy*

"In terms of California . . . we have a very strong commitment towards renewable, both utility scale and distributed generation. Very much motivated by climate change, very much motivated by jobs. . . . Our plan is to look at the barriers, get some experience, and try to get the state ready for sort of a massive rollout as the costs come down. And when we looked at the issues, fundamentally what we found, certainly with the legislature and certainly with the public and local officials, is a real groundswell of support."

—Robert Weisenmiller, *Chairman, California Energy Commission*

"I do see huge pushback from state regulators in terms of allowing utilities to even roll out communication on the distribution network or to install two-way communication meters. They are saying, "We don't see the benefit so we don't want the rates to go up.""

—James Rogers, *Chairman, President and Chief Executive Officer, Duke Energy*

"It's important to understand that this isn't something that can just be simply approved. It's taken us years to get through this process in our jurisdiction. I know there are other jurisdictions that are going through it as well, and maybe some of them have barely even started."

—Rick Morgan, *Commissioner, District of Columbia Public Service Commission*

The overall message at the conference from state energy regulators and public utility commissions on DPS was mixed. Conference participants lamented that while some states are devoting resources to understanding the potential impacts and role of DPS within their jurisdictional purview and are drafting enabling policy around their findings, other states seem to lack awareness, interest, or priority to do so.

Moreover, among states that are actively addressing DPS, their approaches are diverse, and individual policy elements within even a single state may not conform to an internally consistent strategy over time or across sectors. For better or worse, experimentation in DPS policy is widespread in these state "policy labs," and there is some interest emerging in considering the development of model state regulatory frameworks that could be shared within a region or more easily adopted and adjusted for local conditions. For now, with state-level policy key to determining the viability of DPS deployments, those states with the most stable and comprehensive frameworks are receiving the lion's share of DPS investment.

On a role for the U.S. federal government

"One, it reduces the customer acquisition costs for these companies that have these goods and services. . . . Second, it obviously creates market pull, and I think any policy measure that can increase the awareness in the system, without having that burden squarely on the shoulders of the entrepreneurs and the companies, is a step in the right direction."

"When Mayfield decided to make that investment [in SolarCity], it was clear that the ITC for solar was going to get extended to the end of 2016, and so that created a federal, stable policy environment where we thought that the company had ample room to grow not just in California, but across the U.S."

—Pedram Mokrian, *Principal, Mayfield Fund*

"On the federal side, RD&D is just incredibly important."

—Robert Weisenmiller, *Chairman, California Energy Commission*

As described in the chapter, federal government spending on DPS includes loan guarantees, tax credits, accelerated depreciation, and support for research and development. These measures, however, exist alongside a host of competing targeted incentives, rules, and subsidies all across the U.S. energy system. All told, it is difficult to clearly say what the sum financial effect of federal government policy is on DPS deployment relative to the broader energy field.

DPS investors and state regulators emphasized the importance of long-term stability in such federal spending programs in order to arrive at consistent DPS development or regulatory strategies around them. In particular, conference participants highlighted DPS R&D as being particularly suited to federal spending due to its long-term nature, higher risk, and broad base of social beneficiaries (spillovers), but also because of its absolute necessity for future technology development and deployment. Investors also singled out public education on DPS options as a potential role for the federal government in DPS development.

On the net impact of subsidies

"Wind gets \$20–\$23/MWh. That changes where the wind gets deployed. Solar gets up to \$80. Coal gets up to \$120. You may not agree with my logic, but CHP gets \$1.30. Energy efficiency gets nothing. We get all this distortion and we need to recognize the distortion is there."

—Tom Casten, *Chairman, Recycled Energy Development*

"When I think of the cost effectiveness of distributed generation, I don't at all focus on avoided retail costs or retail rates, and the reason is retail rates are full of inefficiencies and subsidies. Having set retail rates for thirty years of my life, I can testify to being guilty of that myself. We create subsidies between classes, commercial versus residential. We create tremendous subsidies and inefficiencies because we don't reflect the time variance at the retail level. We do that for good, political reasons, but, nonetheless, it is inefficient."

—Allen Friefeld, *Executive Vice President, External Affairs, Viridity Energy*

In the absence of well-formed markets that internalize external impacts or other market failures throughout the energy supply chain, local and federal governments have resorted to piecemeal market interventions to address shortcomings as they arise. Conference participants—both regulators and investors—bemoaned the resulting "politically feasible" web of targeted subsidies that vary across technologies, sectors, and geographies. In some cases, subsidies are even created as a counterweight to regulatory failure elsewhere, spending money instead of taking on the task of fixing the policy. This makes investment planning difficult, especially for DPS with its host of technologies, stakeholders, and local conditions.

On end-user rate design choices

"But what are the rate implications? One of our utilities did a plot of where all the DG and EV installations are on their system and the incomes associated with those households. And not surprisingly, those tend to be higher income households that put this in. . . . They're not going on many rented houses, which means a lot of the $40,000 income households are not benefitting from the DG—it's the $140,000. So you have to start saying, with net metering and other programs, 'What are some of the rate impacts of that?'"

—Robert Weisenmiller, *Chairman,
California Energy Commission*

"Rate design is going to become a question of what is the role of a distribution utility? Is it a utility? Can it still have a monopoly relationship with its customers? Can it decide what they put on their house and what they have to pay for?"

"So, two very different approaches, one sort of an exit fee on people who are putting on DG and another saying, 'Look, this is a system resource. Let's charge people across the system for it in a way that helps encourage it, but doesn't disadvantage anybody particularly,' and I think we'll see a lot more of that kind of thing as we go forward."

—Steve Corneli, *Senior Vice President,
Sustainability, Policy, and Strategy, NRG Energy*

State regulators and local utilities are struggling to understand and allocate the equity implications of DPS deployment, especially among residential customers in non-decoupled markets. Their concern is that widespread DPS deployment displaces electricity sales—the main source of utility revenue from residential customers—but customers with DPS who may be paying very little on monthly utility bills still benefit from utility transmission and distribution assets. One approach to this problem has been to institute or increase end-user grid connection charges (similar to the fixed capacity charge that industrial users generally pay) to compensate for a smaller monthly energy charge. The unresolved question is who should pay it.

Steve Corneli of NRG described an example of a regulatory schism now underway as regulators and utilities scramble to respond: San Diego Gas and Electric recently proposed a "network use charge" for only those households with rooftop solar installed, while Austin Energy has proposed raising its monthly base charge on all customers to more accurately address its current infrastructure fixed-costs, with accompanying rate collars to protect the low-income consumers who are less likely to install rooftop solar. While the results of these proposals ultimately turn on state and local law, they illustrate the difference in perspective on the issue of socializing DPS costs.

A particularly tricky related issue is how to structure net metering rates for the customer side of the meter DPS owners who wish to sell back into the grid. Namely, should excess generation be simply deducted from total monthly energy usage, should the utility buy that energy at a set average price, or should the DPS owner see the same real-time electricity pricing as the wholesale market and potentially capture peak rates? Moreover, if a utility is buying power from a DPS end-user, what is a fair allocation of distribution system coordination and the service costs incurred in doing so? Conference participants suggested that the tendency so far has been to pursue logistically and technologically simpler solutions—that is, simple meter deduction or average pricing—especially for small-scale DPS participants. The choices made around net metering structure could, however, significantly impact the form and cost considerations of DPS deployment as well as overall investment efficiency in the electricity system.

CHAPTER 5

POLICY RESEARCH FINDINGS

Given the broad range of applications that DPS technologies serve—from merchant power sales by independent power producers and utility-owned distributed resources to residential systems, waste heat recovery, and emergency backup generation—any attempt to provide a comprehensive analysis of existing policies necessitated outreach to a large number of public- and private-sector entities. The research team conducted qualitative research—interviews and opinion surveys—to obtain input from a variety of stakeholders. In the interests of obtaining frank and accurate feedback, this qualitative research was conducted on the condition of non-attribution.

The research team received inputs from seventy-nine institutions or individuals (by survey or interview) including: federal government (1), state energy departments (5), state public utility commissions (20), investor-owned utilities (15), other utilities/industry entities (6), private developers and financial institutions (13), non-profit organizations (8), and others (11).

The research team designed a questionnaire to solicit the views of the PUCs who play a pivotal role in setting the policy framework for power generation and delivery in the United

States. The survey covered major policy issues surrounding DPS (see Annex 2) and was sent to PUCs in the fifty states and the District of Columbia.[1] Of those sent out, twenty completed surveys were received.

The outreach, through both the interviews and the surveys, aimed to gather respondents' views and opinions on:

- The drivers and benefits of DPS
- The costs and barriers to DPS
- The role of policymakers in DPS
- The effectiveness of DPS-related policy mechanisms
- Other relevant DPS-related trends and issues

5.1 Drivers and Benefits of DPS

Drivers

Participants in the research cited several underlying drivers for greater recent attention to DPS. The most prominent were incentives and mandates that have resulted from environmental policies. In the last decade policymakers have increasingly prioritized the objective of reducing CO_2 emissions, primarily through the promotion of renewable energy resources. The principal policy tools used to promote deployment of these resources are state renewable portfolio standards (RPS) and financial incentives such as tax credits, rebates, loans, and grants. Ambitious RPS initiatives present an increasing challenge to the power industry to meet mandated renewable energy targets, providing a boon to solar, wind, and other zero-carbon generation sources. To the extent that these technologies are deployed at small scale in close proximity to load, RPS can have a direct effect on the deployment of DPS applications. A second and related factor is the declining costs of small-scale generation technologies, such as solar photovoltaic cells and electrochemical fuel cells and storage modules.

Combined with financial incentives, falling technology costs make investments in DPS more attractive relative to centralized sources of generation. The third major driver of recent DPS deployment is constraints on current and future power system assets. At the generation level, uncertainty over the cost and competitiveness of coal and nuclear power plants has left utilities looking for ways to meet increased power demand and reliability requirements while minimizing risk and large-scale capital outlays. With regard to transmission and distribution, system bottlenecks and congestion combined with the difficulty in siting new power lines provide further incentive to locate smaller generation sources nearer to end-users.

Benefits

The majority of DPS benefits cited by respondents to the research were related to their ability to reduce stress on the existing power sector infrastructure. Some respondents saw the primary implication of this benefit as improved system reliability and decreased vulnerability of the grid. For others the implications of this benefit were the ability to offset or defer the costs of new or upgraded generation, transmission, and distribution assets. Others saw DPS as having the potential to reduce the environmental impacts of power generation through avoided large-scale power plant construction, avoided peak operation of existing power plants, and avoided land use for long distance transmission lines. A majority of respondents highlighted the region- and application-specific nature of the benefits of DPS and the need to assess the latter in context.

DPS as a System Asset

Many respondents expressed the view that DPS provide additional resources to an increasingly constrained system, allowing "mitigation of portfolio risk in the long run" in the words of one former PUC chairman. A rural cooperative utility representative said that DPS are viewed as a "resource for dispatch or peak shaving" and that in general renewables were seen as a hedge and part of a broader portfolio. One former PUC commissioner stated that policymakers like DPS for the increased capacity and reliability they provide. A merchant utility indicated that "we think there are synergies on cost and value in deploying DPS that are not easy to realize with more centralized utility scale generation." One IOU said it was "getting much closer to thinking of [DPS] as a resource." A developer saw DPS as a way to mitigate "declining asset utilization" and the "increased peakiness" of the power system—a reference to the greater peak-load demands on the grid and the related requirements to plan around them.

Most Commonly Cited Benefits of DPS

- Reduce vulnerability of the power system
- Provide back-up generation to improve system reliability
- Reduce environmental impacts of power generation
- Offset costs of new or upgraded transmission and generation assets

---

Typical comments across all categories of respondents identified DPS as a resource to avoid or defer transmission or distribution (T&D) investments: "Everywhere there is some long-run marginal cost for power systems that DPS can avoid—it is a system resource," said one respondent.

Increased Efficiency and Security

Others saw the increased deployment of distributed generation and storage as contributing to a more efficient and cost-effective planning process for the distribution system. Rather than the traditional approach that satisfies new load by building capital-intensive (centralized) power plants, these respondents saw DPS as enabling planning to be tailored to the needs of specific distribution circuits. Such an approach has "huge advantages in avoided distribution system costs," said one respondent. Some utilities saw the potential for DPS to reduce load and provide T&D benefits and said they are trying to figure out how to integrate DPS into their planning processes.

> "Everywhere there is some long-run marginal cost for power systems that DPS can avoid—it is a system resource."
>
> —*NGO representative*

When asked about the principal benefits of DPS, most PUC respondents saw significant benefit from reducing the vulnerability of power systems and reducing environmental impacts, with more than half agreeing that these two factors are among the top three benefits. Notably, none of the 20 PUCs participating in our research said that DPS had *no* benefits.

Many participants cited the security-related benefits of DPS, particularly the ability to "hedge" against blackouts and to provide diversity of supply in a system reliant on a limited number of central facilities. The security issue was particularly highlighted by those in the CHP sector.

Regional and Application-Specific Benefits

Some respondents also made a distinction between different modes of DPS deployment when assessing the benefits. According to several IOUs interviewed, one of the difficulties of defining the benefits of DPS is the conflation of two different kinds of application: those on the customer side of the meter that use net metering or other mechanisms to provide a reduction in overall grid-served customer demand, and those small distributed power-supply resources eligible under PURPA to resell their generated power.

"How we look at the benefits of those systems is whether the customer generation is being used to lower the impact to the grid or whether there is an additional resource that needs to be integrated into the system and put into the retail service mix," said one IOU executive.

There was broad consensus among IOUs interviewed that DPS on the customer side of the meter that led to a reduction in end-user demand provided greater predictability and value to the utility than small generators designed to sell power to the utility that had to then resell it to other customers.

One common theme that emerged was the benefits of "localization" that DPS provide. This was mentioned numerous times both in the context of specific benefits of increasing efficiency and reducing costs, but also from a perspective of providing more control over decision-making and resources. An NGO respondent stated that "DPS in general give more local control over how energy is produced and used; whether on a state, municipal, or local level they offer a lot of control . . . relating to long-term assurance of prices and limits them being subject to the whims of regulatory process."

Many respondents (mostly developers), focused on the benefits at the project level. These observers focused on the ability of DPS to provide cost savings for the customer and to address location-specific challenges, such as land-fill reduction through the increased use of biogas. A utility executive observed that once DPS are used to solve an issue on one point in the distribution system the same design can be replicated elsewhere.

Other Notable Comments

- **Job creation:** Several respondents said that DPS can provide job creation; these comments focused on how DPS can provide multiplier effects in the local economy that may be greater than those provided by central power plants. However, PUCs did not share this view; none categorized DPS as having high economic benefits.
- **Market transformation:** Some respondents saw DPS, especially when combined with smart grid innovations such as advanced metering infrastructure, as having the potential to change the way end-users think about their electricity and where it comes from.

5.2 Costs and Barriers

The "barriers" to greater DPS penetration varied according to the interests and affiliation of the respondents. Disagreement between stakeholders over what constituted a barrier—as opposed to a legitimate technical requirement or cost or an issue subject to economic and political preference—provides valuable insight into the challenges facing DPS. The major barriers cited were:

- Costs
- Technical issues
- Lack of policy durability and standardization
- Lack of research and information
- Regulatory framework and the existing utility business model
- The current economic and political climate

Costs

A commonly cited challenge among all respondents—including the overwhelming majority of PUC respondents—was financial cost and cost allocation associated with DPS, whether the upfront costs of the generation assets themselves; the cost of interconnection of generation assets with the existing distribution system infrastructure; or the unknown costs to the power grid of a large addition of DPS capacity to the grid.

The IOUs' focus was on how to limit the impact of the costs of increased DPS penetration on ratepayers, ensure fairness, and take engineering challenges into consideration. In the words of one utility executive: "The number one thing is the cost gap between distributed technologies and the grid price. The solution is not to raise the grid price; this doesn't make economic or political sense." Another utility provided a comment that seemed to bridge the gap in accounting for long term benefits and limiting cost impacts by citing the need for mechanisms to compensate utilities for considering all options on the table.

Utilities, which said that the rate impact of DPS integration is "top of mind," tend to see initiatives that incentivize distributed generation as driving rates upward. IOUs expressed concern that certain programs aimed at incentivizing DPS, such as solar rooftop, result in a subsidization of participants (those who own and operate the solar rooftop systems) by non-participants (those not participating in the DPS program). In such cases, they say, all ratepayers bear the costs of financial incentives, the costs of interconnection, and the costs of possible stranded assets at the distribution level, while only participants benefit.

There was concern among utilities that higher penetration of small-scale generation will mean higher costs of integration—owing to greater system variability—and that these costs will also have to be borne by all ratepayers—both participants and non-participants. In this case, participants receiving the benefits of the distributed energy generation are receiving a subsidy for the installation and/or output of the DPS assets, as well as avoiding the costs associated with connecting their DPS to the grid. These costs are instead borne by the utility and therefore passed on to other customers through higher electricity rates.

> "Somebody needs to do a better job of assessing the whole value of DG."
> —Former state PUC chairman

While customers pay some of the costs of interconnections for most residential DPS applications, these customers are typically subsidized for the capital costs of the technology. Utilities expect increasing political pressure to rate-base these costs (build them into the rates paid by all customers). Depending on the size of the DPS resource and the specific rate structure in place, rate impacts for non-participants can become particularly pronounced.

Although costs for some technologies are decreasing, stakeholders also acknowledged that most DPS technologies are still more expensive than current utility-supplied power (see Chapter 2 for an analysis of the costs of DPS technologies relative to centralized power).

However, many respondents also observed that the full economic benefits of DPS are not well-known and that quantification of the longer-term benefits, in particular, would go a long way to increasing the adoption of such systems.

One former PUC commissioner observed: "In measuring the value of DG, such as offsets on transmission and distribution investments and increased reliability, I never knew what to do with these arguments—somebody needs to do a better job of assessing the whole value of DG." Several respondents said that such an assessment would be of particular value for PUCs, who need a clearer idea of the benefits of greater DPS deployment so they can evaluate whether such systems are in ratepayers' interests.

Several respondents cited the lack of differentiated pricing for power consumption and the lack of the internalization of emissions costs as major barriers to increased DPS deployment. These issues are not related solely to DPS.

Another potential economic barrier raised by one respondent was local permitting costs for DPS, stating, "according to one estimate, the overhead for city and county permitting, zoning, and other regulations and approvals for DPS can add 50 cents per installed watt."

Technical Issues

There was less agreement among respondents around the issues of technical and reliability-related "barriers" of DPS integration. While many developers see interconnection requirements as an obstacle to be overcome through simplification and standardization, many utilities and PUCs maintain that safety and reliability issues necessitate the current requirements.

Many participants pointed out that the fundamental structure and operation of the electric industry presents a technical challenge to deploying more widespread DPS: "the system was simply not designed for a lot of generation on the distribution side," said one respondent. "Power flows in one direction," said another. Power plants and the delivery system were designed to "serve load and that load was not asked to do anything."

Several IOUs pointed out the challenges of integrating an increasing number of distributed generation resources into local circuits. One utility industry representative stated that a "lot of technical engineering is required before benefits can be evaluated let alone implemented." IOUs stressed the importance of ensuring that new DPS systems do not disrupt system reliability for other customers and that they do not adversely "affect the neighbors." Another major technical issue for utilities was the need for communications infrastructure to enable utilities to interact with the growing number of distributed resources. Such communications are necessary, say the IOUs, to enable utilities to accommodate the new generation capacity and to forecast available resources. Several IOUs expressed a desire to see new communications standards to enable such information exchange between distributed resources and the utility.

IOU representatives also said that there was an urgent need for more research and development work on the system impacts of increasing DPS integration, including analysis on the amount of low-cost storage that will be required to smooth out the variation of power output that results from the connection of large amounts of intermittent generators. They admitted that a barrier to such analysis was reluctance among utilities to share technical information.

One particular technical issue raised by both utilities and others was the challenge of interconnecting DPS to the grid (additional comments specific to state-level net metering and interconnection policies are provided in Section 5.4). In the views of the PUC respondents, interconnection requirements are one of the three principal barriers to DPS adoption. This perspective was echoed by several state energy officials, one of whom indicated that "code had yet to be cracked" with regard to the integration of DPS and network distribution systems. An NGO representative noted that "for most customers it does not take much for them to stand down and back off from the utilities and this then gives signals to others to back off."

Many developers said that, despite numerous states having implemented interconnection standards, "utilities can still put up barriers." According to this view, the issue is that utilities are still asking for more—for example, equipment, studies, and other requirements—than might be required in standard agreements. Several expressed the view that utilities' control of the distribution system gave the latter an unfair level of control over the fate of DPS applications. In the words of one: "[Utilities] determine the value proposition. They can kill a project with

standby charges and unnecessary interconnection requirements. It's never a level playing field."

The utility view was different. Utilities cited what they called
legitimate technical concerns, especially the need to change protection schemes for network distribution systems. Several IOUs
observed that the increased prevalence of DPS was likely to cause
complications under existing operating frameworks: existing
IEEE standards, they said, address a single distributed asset in
a system, but do not take account of the aggregate effect of multiple DPS applications. Several utility executives said that this
issue was being exacerbated by a push from states to increase
the limits on the amount of power eligible for net metering.
With megawatt-scale DPS projects being promoted, utilities say
they do not have the technical tools available to understand the
impacts such large generators will have on the overall system:
"Until the 2 MW net metering limits were imposed, we didn't
have any issues with the smaller projects—but once you get
that [net metering] number, you start to see significant issues
with multiple projects proposed on the same 13kv circuit: this
becomes a real issue on how we manage it for our customers."

One utility industry representative noted that the model
interconnection contracts, procedures, and technical requirements in place for small generators were working well. In his
view, the main source of problems between utilities and small
generators relates to the requirements for local disconnects,
indemnification, and utility access to inspect projects.

Lack of Policy Durability and Standardization

A major issue raised throughout our discussions was the need
for consistent and sustained policies. Both public and private

sector respondents expressed the view that policies that vary by jurisdiction, change frequently, or are in place only a short time create an unstable investment environment for businesses, and can be confusing to customers. Study participants called for "policy survivability," "consistency of purpose and vision," greater harmonization of policies, and longer-term implementation of policy tools. This theme was cited widely across the spectrum of respondents. Specific comments included:

- "The technologies are there but the game is so impossible to understand. Clients are planning at three- to five-year business cycles, but tax credits, rebates etc., are changing every couple of years. To move to DPS we need certainty over ten years." (developer)
- "There is market friction: the process with local, state and federal [entities] fitting all these things together is very difficult, especially for small companies to navigate." (venture capital firm)
- "The freeze and thaw approach is not helpful." (NGO)
- "We operate in six states and have six different strategies for DG." (utility)[2]
- "Rules are different across thirty-nine different balancing authorities and fifty states; it's confusing and not uniform." (storage technology company)

There was also a common view that policymakers need to monitor and evaluate policies that *are* in place and to refine them over time to adapt to changing market circumstances. According to this view, there needs to be greater understanding that a policy is not an end in itself, but rather a working guide to meeting overall goals. One respondent noted that there is "a learning curve and [a need to] hammer out details once a policy is in place." For their part, state government officials acknowledge that such fine-tuning of policy and regulation takes time and has to contend with internal processes that are often slower-moving than the market's needs.

Lack of Research and Information

Nearly all respondents cited the lack of research and quantitative data on the costs, benefits, and effects of greater DPS penetration as a barrier. Another frequently cited barrier was the lack of knowledge among—and information exchange between—PUCs, state legislators, and customers regarding DPS technologies. One respondent indicated that the technologies have advanced significantly and, in some cases, costs have come down, but that the regulations in place and the knowledge among major stakeholders to understand the implications of these changes have not kept pace. These challenges were cited prominently by stakeholders in the storage and CHP businesses. Those identified as most in need of more DPS-related information and knowledge were state PUCs, state legislators, and customers. Some illustrative comments include:[3]

- "We need to be able to bring PUCs and legislators up to speed on the technologies and what's available and benefits." (storage technology company)
- "There is a total lack of awareness of CHP at the PUC level—we fight with this all the time." (CHP NGO)
- "What is most important is educating regulators." (IOU)
- "We play a role in providing a layman's version to the legislators. The learning curve is high for customers too: they're not in the business of selling power and sometimes

DG costs more than a car. They are being sold 'savings' and 'being green' but don't have the knowledge yet." (state government energy official)

A related issue is that many institutions, including utilities, state governments, and PUCs, may not have the human and financial capacity to keep pace with advances in DPS technologies and the rapidly changing policy landscape, in particular the goals and timelines established by legislation and other incentives. This is reflected in the challenge for utilities to keep up with applications for interconnection. One state government official noted that, despite net metering and interconnection standards in his state, "utilities have limited resources, and nothing requires them to have the staff for this. Meanwhile utilities are laying off people for reasons with nothing to do with DG."

Regulatory Framework and the Existing Utility Business Model

Many participants cited the existing regulatory framework and business model in the electric industry as a basic barrier to DPS.[4] In states where utility revenues and profits are driven by volume, DPS can be "antithetical" to utilities' interests, representing a loss of sales. There is "very little profit motive for most regulated entities to solve the problems that DPS can address [and they] don't always get rewarded for improving efficiency," said one utility executive. One respondent noted that, "Most utilities don't get a mark-up on purchased power. . . . This makes the utility at best neutral about purchased power if not outright negative."

Another issue raised was that of rate reform; several utilities cited the need for differentiated pricing to send correct signals on scarcity, change behavior, and provide an incentive to invest in better demand-side management technologies.

Several respondents said that many of the regulatory issues related to DPS would not be resolved until there was a decision on whether DPS represent an incremental change in an industry whose basic centralized structure and business model remained intact; or whether DPS are a part of (or perhaps at the forefront of) a major change toward decentralization and a changed role for utilities and customers. A central question, posed by an IOU executive, but echoed elsewhere was: "How is this [distributed] power used—does it go beyond satisfying a customer's need, or go to changing the paradigm and reverse engineering the system?"

Advocates for greater penetration of DPS tended to call into question the traditional power sector mindset that assumes a set level of power demand and then builds generation assets to meet it. As demonstrated in Chapter 2, when viewed in direct comparison with utility-scale generation, some DPS technologies are currently competitive, but most are not. Instead of a direct comparison using the current framework, however, DPS advocates see them as not just a source of power supply, but a part of a bigger "service and systems" approach to power generation and consumption that includes advanced communications and controls, smart grid services, demand-side management, and efficiency. From the utilities' perspective, it was clear that their approach to DPS is determined primarily by whether or not there is a business case—or a profit motive—for the integration of distributed assets.

One issue discussed in our outreach was the impact of deregulation on DPS. Overall, there seemed to be some acknowledgment that generally deregulated markets may be more conducive to DPS. One respondent observed that utility companies in deregulated markets are used to seeing a variety of different players and dealing with competitive forces, which might make them less concerned over the threat of lost revenues posed by DPS. One CHP developer noted that "it is harder to compete with a vertically integrated, traditionally cost-of-service regulated company since they have more to lose."

However, our outreach yielded more comments indicating that the impact on DPS is much more utility-specific (or service-territory specific): "It has more to do with the culture of operating the wire system (and needs on the distribution wires/equipment)." Others stated that some utilities are more supportive because the marginal cost of infrastructure upgrades is so high. One respondent's observation echoes this theme: "Rather than the type of market being relevant, it's more about the utility and its culture, load density, and ownership."

There were some comments reflecting the view that it may be intrinsically easier to deal with public power entities. A few comments reflected this theme: "For municipals and public power, at the distribution level there may be more incentive and influence to implement DPS and renewable energy, but in a larger multistate company, it's hard to see the distribution guys with as much influence."

Current Economic and Political Climate

In addition to these specific issues, two broad external factors were also cited as barriers to increased DPS adoption:

- **The current economic situation:** Developers in particular stated that the current economic recession was hurting the deployment of DPS. Lack of credit and the focus of many businesses on more pressing financial concerns reduced the attractiveness of DPS-related investments and led to a focus on other priorities. One developer observed that larger banks require bigger projects to generate interest, but smaller banks are getting mixed signals to make loans but also to preserve core capital. He added that investors are requiring annual rates of return in the mid-teens on their investments, and that facilities that are normally good candidates that would accept paybacks of five years are not making investments unless the paybacks are less than six months. The current economic situation is also reducing aggregate electricity demand (although, not necessarily peak demand) thus curtailing the motivation to invest in projects that cut energy bills. Another respondent noted that the leveling of demand combined with low natural gas prices was "taking the play away from renewables."

- **Role of government:** The economic recession combined with a more pronounced debate over the role of government in the economy was also raised by several respondents. These participants pointed to the challenge of implementing policy mechanisms in a time of limited financial resources and a focus on reducing government support for a variety of sectors, energy included.

5.3 Policymaker Roles

A fundamental question related to DPS-related policymaking is that of jurisdiction. As Chapter 4 shows, there is a host of policies and regulations in place at the federal, state, and local levels that bear on the deployment and operation of DPS. The research team aimed to determine the views of stakeholders on the appropriate roles for different levels of government.

In general there was a widespread view that there is a role for the federal government to establish a guiding policy framework—a "supportive web of federal policies" in the words of one respondent. Many respondents expressed a preference for a comprehensive federal policy on energy and climate rather than a "patchwork" of state policies, which can vary widely. Such an overarching policy framework would "let utilities or third parties figure out the least-cost path to carbon reduction," in the words of one utility executive. However, most respondents conceded that such comprehensive federal legislation was unlikely to materialize and many private-sector respondents indicated that they are not waiting for this to happen.

Those supportive of the federal government's role in DPS-related policymaking highlighted its ability to "level the playing field" for innovative, emerging technologies through tax policy and to coordinate the standardization of policy and simplify the process of investment in innovation in an effort to create "one big market" for DPS technologies rather than the "fifty different markets" that exist today. An example given of effective federal DPS policy was the provision in the 2005 Energy Policy Act requiring consideration of interconnection standards, which encouraged many states to open dockets to develop such standards.

Some respondents viewed FERC's role in DPS as primarily to remove obstacles to state policy in an effort to create new wholesale markets for renewable and DG. Two areas cited where FERC could play a proactive role were promoting demand response (DR) and energy efficiency (EE) as resources and encouraging price signals from wholesale markets to be passed through to retail rates.[5] More than one respondent said that the promotion of "price responsive demand" (PRD) provides a model for valuing and incorporating the benefits of DPS.[6]

At the federal level, PUCs see primary responsibility for DPS promotion as resting with the Department of Energy in the form of increased R&D support and to improve the cost effectiveness of DPS technologies. PUCs saw little or no role for the Federal Energy Regulatory Commission (FERC) or the Environmental Protection Agency in DPS promotion.

A majority of respondents also indicated that the states are particularly well-suited to design and implement policy for DPS. Many respondents expressed the view that, given their greater knowledge about resource bases, customer profiles and concerns, and system designs and constraints, states were more likely than federal administrators to promote effective changes at the distribution level. Supporting this theme, one participant mentioned that, given the complexity of the issues involved, constant dialogue and communication were required among customers, utilities, developers, state PUCS, and other stakeholders to ensure the most effective hands-on policy development, implementation, monitoring, and refinement.

There were also several comments supporting the idea of "state as laboratory," in which states take the initiative in policy implementation and lead by example. As one observer noted, "absent federal legislation, states are more inclined to compete with each other."

While there was broad support for the states as primary DPS policymakers, several groups of stakeholders interviewed highlighted what they saw as competing—and sometimes contradictory—objectives of state and local policymakers with regard to DPS deployment. In the words of one IOU executive, several state incentives, which form the basis of developer products and end-user business plans and investment decisions, are put in place "without a very well-defined policy framework for how IOUs respond to what the market place is offering." There was particular criticism of states that "are incentivizing a technology, but not putting in place a policy framework that assesses the best use of that technology or what is the best use of the technology at this stage of its development." Utilities also noted the fundamental tension between the use of increasingly scarce state funds to incentivize DPS and the political reluctance to see increases in electricity rates, and the legal difficulties that state DPS policies sometimes face with regard to federal law. Such policy friction is not only found between the state and federal governments. One mayor interviewed explained how his city had organized a solar rooftop initiative only to find it blocked by state officials on the grounds that it contravened competition laws aimed to protect the incumbent power provider. The city got around the issue by leasing the rooftop solar panels from a third party.

Given the pivotal role of states in DPS policymaking, respondents frequently highlighted the unique role of the state utility regulatory commissions. Many respondents saw the commissions as important actors on this issue, but also outlined the unique challenges confronting them. These include the need to maintain an up-to-date familiarity with the regulatory and technical aspects of DPS, as well as the need to balance ratepayer and system benefits. A common observation was that PUCs have to accommodate the regulatory imperative of keeping costs down while accommodating policies that drive prices up. In the words of one IOU executive, "policy is legislation-driven and regulators are stuck in middle." A venture capital firm representative highlighted the power of PUCs to determine the commercial success of DPS investments. He said he advises clients to treat the PUCs as their financially conservative CFO, with the power to decide where to spend money and a very low appetite for risk.

5.4 Policy Mechanisms

A major objective of the primary research effort was to canvass the views of power sector stakeholders on the range of existing and proposed policy mechanisms impacting DPS. An assessment of the effectiveness of existing DPS-related policy mechanisms is complicated by two factors: the respondent's perception of the benefits, objectives, and potential of DPS; and the difficulty of isolating the effect of a single policy mechanism in a system with numerous incentives, standards, and rules—enforced by different levels of government—simultaneously in place.

Financial Incentives

There was a general sentiment that financial incentives are important and play a key role in helping to "pull" innovative and early stage technologies to greater commercialization. Of all the specific policy mechanisms suggested in the survey, "tax incentives for purchase and installation" were overwhelmingly seen by PUCs as the most effective means of increasing DPS, with all respondents describing it as very or somewhat effective.

Tax Credits, Grants, and Rebates

There were generally supportive comments toward tax credits and incentives such as the ITC and PTC, as well as loan programs. Such incentives were seen to be effective in addressing the cost barriers for nascent DPS technologies. One utility investing in solar PV distributed generation noted that the combination of federal and state policies such as loan guarantees, tax credits, grants, and an RPS plus power purchase agreements (PPAs), "makes it possible to invest in solar, and where [such incentives] exist, we invest." Some comments focused on the transaction costs of specific financial incentives, with one respondent preferring grants to tax incentives to avoid losses to "middle men." Another respondent reported having to hire five extra staff to fill in all the documentation required for a DOE loan guarantee.

There was a widespread view that financial mechanisms needed to be "smarter," especially in the current atmosphere of spending cuts and calls for a reduced role for government. The most common view in this regard was the need for financial incentives to address a wider variety of commercialization stages and to be phased out over time as a technology becomes more commercially deployed. The challenge for one utility representative was how to "have smart subsides that leverage private financing but have minimal impact on federal government."

There were also several views that were cautious or outrightly critical of this category of policy tools. Most of these comments noted concerns of cost and policy durability and variation by jurisdiction. They noted that the current economic and political environment makes it increasingly challenging to justify and sustain these mechanisms and that federal and state cost-cutting put these policies "hugely at risk." Even if they do survive, the uncertainty around fiscal incentives was seen as a barrier in itself.

Others were critical of the fundamental case for ongoing financial incentives. "If there is an institutional barrier to deploying a technology that otherwise makes good economic sense, then remove the barrier—don't use other incentives to promote it," said one PUC commissioner. Some respondents saw the job of incentives as exploiting economies of scale to get certain technologies to competitiveness as quickly as possible, while others thought that they should be "technology neutral."

Feed-In Tariffs

There was broad skepticism among respondents toward the feasibility and effectiveness of feed-in tariffs as a policy tool. There was recognition that FITs can provide a predictable revenue stream and that they can be a very useful short-term instrument to spur certain technologies. Several participants also said that there was an increasing interest in FITs and that "incentivizing utilities to launch a robust FIT could be a game changer." However, the preponderance of views was that FITs were politically difficult to implement and difficult to manage. Notably, the PUCs' enthusiasm for the effectiveness of tax incentives did not extend to FITs, which they saw as significantly less effective.

Many of those critical of FITs outlined two major drawbacks: the difficulty in determining the price paid for the power generated, and the challenge of determining when to phase out subsidies. It was evident from many of the responses that the current political environment and history of the U.S. power sector played a major role in the negative views expressed. "We did this [before] and it was called PURPA: it might help in the short-term but the politics are ugly," said one respondent. Other criticisms of FITs revolved around objections to paying more than necessary for output and the danger of FITs leading to the creation of "zombie industries." There was particular concern expressed about the impact of FITs on the economics of technologies not included in the FIT program, whose competitiveness is in danger of being undermined by generous subsidies to their rivals.

There also were concerns over the short-term nature of this mechanism, as well as over whether it was the best market-based tool available. One respondent referred to FITs as "training wheels" that need to come off. Others noted that FITs are "not a long-term solution . . . likely to create a feeding frenzy and then go away"; and that "ITC [investment tax credits] and some type of mandate are better than FITs."

A less strident view and one that chimed with the need for "smarter" policies, was that FITs can be tailored to meet some goals and can be designed in such a way as to be appropriate for specific technologies at specific stages of their development. According to this view, FITs are appropriate for very early-stage technologies such as storage, but are not appropriate for the creation of long-term stable markets for more developed technologies. For the latter, it was suggested that programs such as a reverse auction market, through which developers compete to offer bids for projects, were more effective.

Rules and Regulations

Mandates

Respondents' view on mandates such as renewable portfolio standards (RPS) was mixed. There was acknowledgment that RPS can play a role in supporting greater renewable energy and DPS penetration in the market, but that this mechanism needs to be smarter and better targeted.

One of the main objections to mandates was that they involve too much government intervention and restrict the potential of market forces. One developer noted that, "A national RPS, in our view, is biased to politically-favored technologies and is not based on performance-based standards." A municipal utility official commented that, "Mandates become a government-approved appropriate number and stifle the market's ability to find something better."

> On FITs: "We did this [before] and it was called PURPA: it might help in the short-term but the politics are ugly."
> —*Utility executive*

Several suggestions for improving the effectiveness of mandates focused on expansion of the renewable energy credit (REC) market to include a broader range technologies and approaches and closer monitoring of the appropriateness of RPS targets. One respondent noted that there was a need to reduce the volatility of REC prices: "We work in a world of 15 year projects, but who knows what prices and the market are going to be like that far out." Another commented that there is too much ambiguity surrounding REC ownership and that "few states have addressed where RECs go."

There were several comments suggesting that RPS may not be sufficiently targeted or address a broad enough spectrum of challenges, such as the need for investment in the grid. Some respondents also questioned the effectiveness of RPS for increasing penetration of specific technologies: if increased solar deployment is the goal, said one respondent, it would be better to use a specific solar policy (or set of policies) rather than an RPS to achieve it.

Net Metering and Interconnection

Adoption of uniform interconnection standards was the second most effective policy in the views of the PUC respondents, with all but two seeing the measure as being very or somewhat effective in increasing DPS penetration. Net metering was also identified by the majority of the PUCs as having the most potential to overcome rate-related impediments to increased DPS penetration.

The general sentiment among other respondents was that while there has been significant progress in implementing net metering and interconnection policies across the states, the policies need to be revised and updated to keep pace with technical and market developments. Several comments noted a lack of uniformity, arbitrariness of certain regulations, and concerns about cost and rate impacts.[7]

Developers were more likely to criticize what they saw as lack of uniformity in net metering limits. "It appears that rules arbitrarily pick a size you can net meter on up to 2 MW or 5 MW, but why can't it be whatever is required?" said one CHP developer. To better determine the limits on net metering, some stakeholders suggested reassessing utility peak demand to determine current load levels. According to this perspective, net metering caps based on historic levels may not reflect the full potential of load centers to absorb additional distributed generation. Another suggestion for making net metering caps more location-specific was giving PUCs and local regulators the discretion to set higher program caps, or to set net metering caps based on a percentage of peak load, rather than a fixed limit. The view from the PUCs on net metering focused more on the adequacy of current net metering arrangements to cope with large projects. This was echoed by one NGO respondent who commented that net metering was created to simplify the process for small scale generation and that, "More significant flows should be governed by commercial agreements."

Similar systems-related concerns were expressed by IOUs and PUCs about interconnection standards. Utility executives said that current IEEE standards did not make provision for the current level of distributed resources on a circuit. One PUC commissioner described as a "major challenge" the connection of DPS to a network distribution system with multiple feeders.

This issue was also raised by a developer, who observed that existing standards were devised with assumptions about upper limits on distributed generation capacity, which may be surpassed as levels of DPS penetration increase.

Many IOU respondents focused on the costs associated with interconnection and net metering, and the impacts on ratepayers. A recurring theme was that of equity for non-participants (ratepayers not part of the net metering program), who are seen as often having to pay for interconnection costs through the rate base. One IOU indicated that for net-metered systems over 2 MW there is increased pressure to rate-base higher interconnection costs. Another IOU seconded this comment noting that with declining usage and the increased cost of integration, "unit costs have started to explode." In short, IOUs stressed that for those systems under 1MW (and those serving their own load), costs and broader ratepayer impacts are not a major issue. However, as more customers begin selling power back to the grid, stranded distribution costs and interconnection costs rise. In addition, the move to expand the adoption of virtual net metering, and thus create larger systems, will also add to pressure for higher prices.

There were several comments noting the important role PUCs have in ensuring appropriate net metering and interconnection standards. However, there was some doubt expressed over the ability of PUCs to fulfill this role. While some commissions have tried to standardize net metering and interconnection regulations, one respondent expressed the view that "it is not a high priority for PUCs to push back against a utility's safety argument." A state government energy official mentioned that while PUCs had a role in establishing clearer standards or eliminating unnecessary requirements, "it's hard to imagine the commission being the judge—it's not accustomed to handling this."

One observer noted that utilities are used to connecting a handful of very large generators with long lead times for construction and that such connections have not been detrimental to systems planning. However, now that more distributed generation systems are coming online, the challenge is how to efficiently interconnect all these systems in cost effective way—for smaller systems interconnection costs can represent a large portion of total costs[8]—while ensuring reliability and safety. One policy change proposed is to raise the fast track screen threshold to ensure that smaller systems can proceed in a reasonable time frame.

Rate-related Mechanisms

The research aimed to solicit respondents' views on the effectiveness of rate-related mechanisms for increased penetration of DPS. Two such mechanisms that were prominently highlighted were "decoupling" and "dynamic pricing." Decoupling—the process of breaking the link between the volume of electricity sold and the revenues of utilities—was identified by many respondents as an effective policy tool for DPS promotion.

Almost half of the states in the United States currently have decoupling or a similar revenue adjustment mechanism in place to address the issue of "lost revenue" and to allow a utility to recover its fixed costs even when sales revenues are lower than projected.

Decoupling was identified by many respondents as an effective policy tool for DPS promotion.

Decoupling was seen as an important driver of energy efficiency and a helpful tool in removing utilities' financial disincentives to adopt new sources of generation by "putting the minds of [their] accountants at ease." However, while decoupling takes away the disincentive associated with the loss of revenue associated with DPS, it was seen by at least one utility-industry representative as offering no incentive or reward to promote DPS. Others were more skeptical of decoupling. A PUC official said that most decoupling is an artifact of having distribution rates based on 19th century technologies: "We should design more cost-based distribution rates and with AMI [advanced metering infrastructure] this will become possible."

Dynamic pricing—the differentiation of electricity pricing according to the relative cost of delivery—was the second rate-related mechanism that respondents saw as having potential to increase the penetration of DPS. PUCs identified it as the second most effective method (after net metering) to address rate-related impediments to DPS.

Advocates of dynamic pricing saw its value in making customers aware of the cost of power they consume and produce, and in providing justification for incentives for resources such as DPS that can help to address high peak load.

Several participants indicated that dynamic pricing is particularly important for solar deployment: "Unless you begin to value solar as a peaking resource, there's a big challenge in pushing for distributed solar. If you start to get prices at peak, you'll see a difference."

While there was enthusiasm for the effectiveness of dynamic pricing, several participants highlighted the political challenges of implementing such a mechanism, saying that PUCs would not be likely to make such pricing mandatory owing to the potential impact on ratepayers.

Strategies and Targets

Carbon Pricing

As noted above, many respondents believed that some form of overarching, comprehensive federal legislation would be very helpful in creating a transparent investment climate for DPS. There was general agreement that a price on carbon is needed and would benefit DPS deployment, but little expectation that this policy mechanism would be established any time soon. Most respondents agreed with the need for a price on carbon both as an appropriate role of the federal government as well as to establish broad, directional policy guiding the energy sector. However, one exception to this observation was the view that any comprehensive federal policy would carry the risk of retarding climate-related efforts of progressive states in favor of a compromise to reach national agreement.

5.5 Other Major DPS-Related Issues

In addition to the issues discussed above, stakeholders identified three applications they saw as being particularly important to a discussion on the future of DPS.

Combined Heat and Power (CHP)

One of the major themes emerging in our outreach was the lack of knowledge of CHP and its benefits and consequently the lack of policy recognition given to it at all levels. This is commensurate with the views and findings of advocacy groups and other NGOs tracking the status and role of the CHP industry. For example, in a forthcoming analysis, the American Council for an Energy-Efficient Economy (ACEEE) states:

> Few state energy offices and public service commissions prioritize CHP. CHP is often viewed by its advocates and supporters as a "homeless" suite of technologies in public policy. CHP is not well understood by regulators, not well-suited for renewable energy programs—because it is often powered by non-renewable fuels—and too expensive for most short-term energy efficiency programs because its payback period is long and its upfront costs high compared to many other efficiency measures.[9]

The idea of CHP as a "homeless" technology was echoed in interviews with many stakeholders. Respondents noted that the problem begins with a lack of knowledge of CHP systems—what they are and how they work—as well as the potential benefits.

Many cited the struggle in implementing specific CHP policies, or having CHP treated on an equal basis with energy efficiency or renewable energy. One NGO summarized the challenges in working with one state government to carve out a place for CHP either in the energy efficiency resource standard or the RPS: "The energy efficiency constituency believes that CHP does not qualify as energy efficiency, or reducing load within a given facility. . . . The renewable energy crowd doesn't see CHP as renewable since 'it's just another fossil fuel power plant.' And utilities say you generate power but you're too small, so you're not a utility power plant."

Despite the perceived lack of recognition for CHP, many respondents highlighted the environmental, efficiency, and energy security benefits of the technology. They noted that CHP combines many of the benefits that come with distributed assets (small capital cost, location close to load, avoided transmission and distribution costs) with the reliability of a centralized power station, the added security benefit of being able to operate independently of the grid, and greatly superior efficiency.

Some respondents said that CHP had been overlooked due to a preoccupation among policymakers for "being green and giving incentives to wind and solar." Others noted that some specific CHP-related policies and incentives are being implemented at the state level (albeit unevenly) but that CHP is not included in most state RPS or EERS, meaning that it was not being fully rewarded for the thermal benefits it provides.[10]

Several participants discussed the particular challenges involved in recognizing the environmental benefits of CHP. These comments noted the need to look at a "system-wide emissions profile," especially in terms of providing credit to CHP's thermal benefits in lowering emissions. The need for output-based emissions standards was specifically highlighted in this regard.

Storage

Stakeholders in our outreach reiterated the view that innovation and greater deployment of storage could significantly enhance overall operational efficiency of the existing electricity system. Storage was identified as "emissions-free capacity," a source of "time value," and "a great way to make an intermittent resource more valuable." As a generation asset, storage was recognized by some respondents as a "vastly superior" resource, owing to its continuous synchronization, its ability to idle without burning fuel, and to operate without being shut off.

Many issues pertaining to generation-related aspects of DPS were also mentioned in relation to storage including high costs and the need to value the benefits.

There were several comments noting that storage remains a new concept for many stakeholders, especially lawmakers and PUCs. Some respondents commented that in most cases the technology is relatively new or quickly evolving and it takes time for people to catch up to understanding the technologies and their applications and implications. While batteries, flywheels, compressed air energy storage (CAES), and thermal-storage technologies have been around for a long time, many respondents said that there was a lack of understanding of the extent to which such applications have improved in performance. Others saw it as "only a matter of time before storage gets its due in policy circles."

The other major challenge for storage—and one that echoes previous comments on DPS generally—is the categorization and quantification of its benefits. Several participants commented on the fact that storage does not fit neatly into a category or is often poorly defined, mainly due to the fact that it is "really several technologies that have their own cost-benefits" and applications. One respondent noted the transmission benefits of storage, but asked, "If you rate-base it as a transmission asset, do you disadvantage it for other services?" Others said that the difficulty in quantifying storage was that there was "no single methodology for valuing it" because its value was so systems-specific.

A storage technology company executive echoed the challenge in valuation of storage benefits and specifically in getting utilities to do a thorough cost-benefit analysis, stating that in a few cases, utilities are not giving credit for transmission and distribution investment deferral, but that "1 MW at the socket is more valuable than at generation." He said that one of the key questions in storage is: "What are you valuing and how?"

One respondent pointed out that FERC traditionally has tended to think in terms of generation, transmission, and distribution; but with storage sometimes acting as a generator and sometimes a transmission asset, it is trying to re-think this. Another commented that FERC is examining how to provide compensation for fast regulation (short-term balancing of load) and how to treat storage as a transmission asset to address local congestion issues.[11]

Participants generally recognized that the lack of knowledge of storage technologies and their benefits contributes to the lack of movement to develop regulations to support deployment. The lack of clarity around how to categorize storage has led to a fragmented approach to related policy and regulations, with some states treating storage as generation, some allowing storage in an RPS, and others considering it as eligible for peak demand reduction standards.

There were several recommendations on how to improve this situation. One respondent suggested that storage policies needed to be tailored to specific applications rather than technologies: "Perhaps a battery system should be rate-based by the utility, but customers could sell regulation services to the market." To determine the monetary benefits of storage, one respondent advocated the development of a utility-specific calculator that would provide information on the real value of storage at the transmission or end-user level: "These types of tools make it very transparent in evaluating new distribution investments versus storage. Any PUC where there is a large metro area with load pockets is looking at these calculators."

A final suggestion endorsed by several respondents was the modification of financial incentives such as investment tax credits to make it clear where storage was eligible for support.

Smart Grid

Across the spectrum of participants it was widely acknowledged that the smart grid plays a major role in supporting greater penetration of DPS. Many noted that the smart grid and related control and information systems will make it easier to integrate DPS into the power grid. In particular, some respondents saw the smart grid as a central factor in "rooting out the old system," and facilitating the move to greater local control over production and demand, and a more efficient use of energy.

Smart meters or AMI (advanced metering infrastructure) and smart appliances were both viewed as having the potential to play a significant role in transitioning toward more informed end-users and more dynamic pricing of power, which would increase the appeal of DPS.

One participant noted microgrids as a system for bringing more resources into the distribution system. This participant stated that the complexity of higher penetration of distributed energy resources "leads us to physically push toward microgrids" as a system to facilitate bringing more resources into the distribution system. "With this complexity, we can't solve the problem without breaking it into a microgrid. Think of the microgrid as a tool within the smart grid."

Expert Forum

"Neither our state governments nor federal government can really afford subsidies. We're not in that period in history. There is adequate public/private capital that can go to work in these areas if the incentives are right."

"I think distributed generation in some senses of the phrase is the same threat to central station—not a complete threat— as you see tablets and smartphones being a threat to the PC."

—James Rogers, *Chairman, President and Chief Executive Officer, Duke Energy*

"How do we get the homeowner, the shopkeeper, the CFO, the housewife, to say this is a good investment for me today? And then policymakers, on the other hand, have got to say this is good for the nation, not over forty years but over the next five or ten."

—Andrew Karsner, *Executive Chairman, Manifest Energy*

As described in this study, there are many stakeholders affected by DPS deployment. But ultimately whatever the regulations or subsidies or strategic goals or technological attractiveness, consumer interest and willingness to buy or use DPS technology is clearly needed in order for it to succeed. Potential DPS participants on the buy- or sell-side range from the "cold beer, hot shower" residential end-user to entrepreneurial system developers, from investor-owned utilities themselves to base commanders in the armed forces: Who sees value to DPS, and how will their demand shape its development? Conference participants debated if DPS deployment would be pushed from the top-down to achieve an anticipated system-wide social benefit, or if it would be pulled from individual end-users at the bottom who want it faster than they can get it.

The end-user perspective

"The average consumer's cost of electricity is 1.9 percent of their disposable income, the lowest it's been in fifty years. And so they wake up in the morning and say they don't worry about it."

—Andrew Karsner, *Executive Chairman, Manifest Energy*

"The really killer app in order to bring about distributed energy resources is to get the pricing right. Right now the customer does not see the true value of the electricity at any given time. . . . It's just like going into a grocery store and filling up your cart and paying for it by weight. And that's the way we pay for electricity in this country."

—Rick Morgan, *Commissioner, District of Columbia Public Service Commission*

"There's going to be a lot more DG and DPS because the costs are coming down. As SolarCity is doing, people are buying these because they're cheaper, not because they think it's the right thing, not because they are concerned about melting icecaps or because they're concerned about energy security, but because it's cheaper, and, oh, by the way, it looks pretty cool on somebody's house to be able to say, 'I'm independent, I'm making my own energy, and it's clean.'"

—Steve Corneli, *Senior Vice President, Sustainability, Policy, and Strategy, NRG Energy*

"Whether it's one of these embedded gas-powered usually neighborhood-type systems or a commercial system, people have said, 'Hey, look, the interruptions have become so frequent that, because of severe weather events, I'm just going to go ahead and make the investment because the loss of economic good or end quality of life just makes it so imperative that I insure myself.' I think as we see more and more opportunities come for 'beyond–fossil-fuel' types of power generation systems and the kinds of storage systems that can really, really leverage those, we're going to see a lot more of a bottom up demand for distributed power systems."

—Dennis McGinn (Vice Admiral, Retired), *President, American Council on Renewable Energy*

Because DPS are smaller scale and situated closer to the end of the energy supply system, they are generally more relevant to end-users than conventional energy supply infrastructure. In some cases the energy user may actually be making the DPS infrastructure purchase decision, such as when individuals or companies purchase a rooftop solar system or a backup fuel cell. Even if not making the capital outlay, end-users can still be affected by the DPS application's cost, financing, performance, reliability, and image. Consumers may even be asked to adjust their own behaviors to fit DPS technology characteristics, which is difficult.

Some conference participants expressed concern that day-to-day DPS cost savings may not be a strong enough motivation for residential end-users to deal with the complexity of installing and maintaining a system, but that DPS could nevertheless be attractive to these buyers for other reasons such as backup reliability.

The developer perspective

> "In terms of the utility solicitations, the ratio again is 10–20 to 1 between the amount they're trying to buy and the bids they're getting."
>
> —Robert Weisenmiller, *Chairman, California Energy Commission*
>
> "The question here is, 'Do you want distributed generation to succeed?,' as opposed to, 'Do you want it to succeed with the stuff I'm selling?'"
>
> —Andrew Karsner, *Executive Chairman, Manifest Energy*

Independent power project developers are deploying DPS at various scales, from individual residential installations to commercial projects and larger systems on domestic military bases. DPS developers are implementers: they use end-user cash purchase, equipment lease, or power purchase agreement financing models to procure DPS products from vendors, to install systems, and to offer end-users retail DPS packages that may include product, maintenance, and financing or billing. Private capital for these transactions is often supported by monetization of various federal and state subsidies. For residential or commercial end-users who elect to use DPS for their homes or businesses, project developers can make the process easier and more accessible.

Conference participants discussed how developers are taking a major role in helping to create a functional market for DPS technologies by facilitating information flow and commercial relationships across stakeholders. Developers also educate consumers, helping to make their energy use choices more salient. These actors end up being a major driver of broad DPS deployment as their revenue is directly tied to the number of systems they are able to help implement.

The vendor, technology entrepreneur, and early-stage investor perspective

> "What really kind of saved us in the Montreal Protocol was the fact that DuPont came along with an invention that was not expensive, that people could use, and that made a big contribution to having it work. I must say I think in the current context getting the pot stirred here, we're going to see things come along and probably they're going to come along in part from industry."
>
> —George P. Shultz, *Thomas W. and Susan B. Ford Distinguished Fellow, The Hoover Institution*

The DPS market that exists today was predicated on the emergence of new technologies that singly or taken together can now substitute for or complement conventional power systems, and which, importantly, can be sold at some profit. As early-stage investment and development continues to introduce new DPS products, and as manufacturing scale drives down costs (and, potentially, margins) of more mature technologies, DPS vendors, entrepreneurs, and investors are hoping that growth in acceptance of and demand for DPS products is able to match increasing competitiveness in market supply.

The utility perspective

"There are some utilities that are embracing distributed power systems; others are not so sure and they're moving more slowly. We, as regulators, are finding ourselves needing to do some nudging in many cases to move the utilities toward a more modern expansive view of the electrical grid because there are so many potential benefits from doing that."

—Rick Morgan, *Commissioner, District of Columbia Public Service Commission*

"What we have chosen to do is basically incorporate it in our model.... We went to our regulator, we asked for permission ... and we did the installation. We tried to cut that 50 percent cost. ... We did cut that cost and we have a very low cost to capital."

On Duke Energy installing 10 MW of residential and commercial rooftop PV: "The reason we did it is, one, to establish the precedent that we could be in that business, in a sense extending our business model. But secondly, we wanted to learn how to operate in a world where you have distributed intermittent power across your system."

"I think the natural economics of what's going to occur over the next several decades will create a huge opportunity for distributed generation in the U.S. and we need to embrace it as a utility company. And I do think that we can both compete in terms of building distributed generation within the homes and businesses of our customers, or we can cooperate with those who have lower cost to capital."

—James Rogers, *Chairman, President and Chief Executive Officer, Duke Energy*

"I think that the role of the utility is going to need to be more focused on facilitating customer choices and less about making choices on behalf of customers because technology is just at a point where we can do this."

—Kevin Fox, *Interstate Renewable Energy Council*

DPS force the issue of the role of traditional "natural monopoly" IOUs in a modern power system. Conference participants described how DPS are already fulfilling real needs in the electric system: various forms of distributed generation are approaching the avoided cost to otherwise expand or replace centralized power stations; DPS can reduce the need for new long-distance transmission investment; and, DPS can even provide crucial grid and load services.

Considering such DPS roles, IOUs are examining the responsibilities, opportunities, and incentives in this growth space. Access to very low cost of capital and a lack of large-scale investment opportunities in markets with slow electricity demand growth has driven interest among some IOUs in deploying and owning DPS systems themselves. Utility investment areas include distribution, advanced metering, grid communications, and in some cases, even the distributed generation assets themselves. Other IOUs see DPS as a technical or operational burden for grid coordination or worry that the investments required to upgrade distribution and metering infrastructure will not be accepted into their rate base.

The military perspective

"And at the end of the day, every investment that we make somehow needs to add to three things: combat capability, combat capability, and combat capability for the military. Otherwise it's an investment we probably shouldn't be making."

"We have to make some well-placed bets out there, but we also have to have milestone points where we look at it again and go if this isn't panning out well, then let's stop that investment so we make a good prudent use. But we do have to be able to think ten and twenty years out because I think that's what you demand of us as taxpayers, and you should demand that of us."

> —Vice Admiral Philip Cullom, *Director, Energy and Environmental Readiness Division, U.S. Navy*

"How the department gets innovation isn't just the R&D that we sponsor directly. Our acquisition budget is hundreds of billions of dollars a year and that's where the big money is. And if we start putting requirements in our acquisitions for better energy performance, that's also an R&D draw and that is one place where we're going to improve no matter what our budget cuts look like. We are going to make those requirements and that will stimulate R&D as well."

> —Sharon Burke, *Assistant Secretary of Defense for Operational Energy Plans and Programs, U.S. Department of Defense*

"Recycled energy or waste energy recovery . . . is really, really good for our bottom line."

> —Dennis McGinn (Vice Admiral, Retired), *President, American Council on Renewable Energy*

As described in the study, the armed forces are major direct purchasers of DPS technologies such as backup ICE generators and turbines, batteries, and mobile solar panels for use on bases or in theater. Individual services are also entering into end-user lease or production purchase agreements with DPS project developers to deploy larger-scale DPS on bases (making the projects eligible for federal government subsidies) and working with civilian utilities to develop secure base microgrids.

The military also funds DPS research and development through grants and prizes targeting early-stage technology development and demonstrations that could contribute to mission objectives but which also have wider civilian applicability. Though R&D and infrastructure spending will likely be a target for cost cutting with anticipated Department of Defense budget cuts of approximately $450 billion over the next 10 years, the military will continue to support both direct DPS R&D and indirect market development through its massive procurement spending that will likely incorporate DPS concepts into relevant product requirements.

Military spending on DPS and other emerging technologies is an interesting laboratory; conference participants noted that though investment and operational decisions are principally guided by return-on-investment, costs and benefits are specially valued in consideration of mission objectives. For example, while monetary costs and benefits basically align with civilian markets, the military must also give special consideration to mission capability, security, and human life while operating in unique or extreme operational and tactical conditions. This affects the calculus of investing in and deploying various DPS technologies and so can sometimes economically support DPS development in ways that the civilian market alone cannot.

CHAPTER 6

CONCLUSIONS
AND RECOMMENDATIONS

6.1 Summary of Findings

Economics of DPS

As the previous chapters demonstrate, distributed power systems comprise many technologies and applications. Advances in technology, coupled with—and sometimes driven by—policies to support smaller scale, more localized generation of electricity have led to a situation in which the economics of some DPS applications have improved rapidly. However, using a direct cost-comparison model, DPS technologies are, in general, still less cost-competitive than most coal and gas-fired central-station generation alternatives. Those DPS technologies that are cost-competitive on a per-MWh basis require central station generation avoided-cost assumptions that include higher-priced fuel (natural gas at up to 7.50/MMBtu) and regions with high levels of system congestion, planned grid investment, and no excess generation capacity. The DPS technologies that are cost-competitive under these circumstances are IC engines and gas turbines with

CHP, and medium- and community-scale wind. Other technologies that are nearly cost-competitive with the higher cost range of central fossil-fuel power generation are fuel cells, medium-sized (2–5 MW) solar photovoltaic, and microturbine CHP.

Results show that the economic benefits of DPS are location- and time-specific. Economic analysis assuming a moderate carbon price of $30/ton would increase the competitiveness of some renewable energy DPS applications, with large-scale solar competitive with both coal and gas in some circumstances. Electric fuel cells and medium-scale solar applications approach competitiveness with the upper range of coal-fired power in this scenario. However, even with a moderate carbon price in place, many current DPS technologies are still not cost-competitive with most central-station generation.

The economics of DPS technologies relative to central power generation will change over time. Quantifying the current competitiveness of DPS represents a single point in time: many DPS technologies are realizing rapid decreases in unit cost that are likely to continue as research, development, and deployment continue. While advances have also been made in the efficiency of centralized power generation, the rate of such advances is generally accepted to be lower than that of many DPS technologies, particularly solar and wind.

Costs, Benefits, and Barriers

The economic analysis presented in Chapter 2 defines the benefits of DPS in terms of avoided costs (including generation, transmission, and distribution), which is a standard industry cost-comparison. However, according to many stakeholders across the electric power industry interviewed in the course of this study, DPS provides benefits that are not currently captured by existing economic models. Such benefits include improved efficiency of the distribution system, environmental and land-use benefits, possible job-creation benefits, and other region-specific benefits. They also include the security value of DPS, both as a means of decreasing the vulnerability of the civilian grid to disruption and attack and as a resource for the base and theater operations of the U.S. military. The full costs of realizing the claimed potential benefits of DPS are unknown. Utilities, regulators, and engineers point to the increasing financial burden of connecting new DPS systems and to the unknown technical and safety consequences of integrating large amounts of distributed assets to today's grid infrastructure which was designed for one-way distribution of power. Advocates of DPS, such as developers, point to a range of barriers—mostly technical—to greater deployment and realization of the potential benefits.

Two points of near-universal agreement among all stakeholders are: (1) there is lack of familiarity with many aspects of DPS; and, (2) there is insufficient information exchange among regulators, policymakers, and power sector entities.

Policies

There is a large, and increasing, number of policies in place both at the state and federal levels that directly and indirectly impact DPS adoption. According to the majority of respondents interviewed for this study, the primary responsibility for DPS policymaking should be at the state level, although the federal government should have a role in setting a foundational energy policy framework.

Major Findings and Conclusions

1. DPS technologies are, in general, still less cost competitive than most centralized generation alternatives.

2. The economic benefits of DPS are location- and time-specific.

3. A moderate price on carbon would increase the competitiveness of some renewable energy DPS applications.

4. Many DPS technologies are realizing rapid decreases in unit cost that are likely to continue as research, development, and deployment continue.

5. DPS provides benefits that are not currently captured by existing economic models.

6. The full costs of realizing the claimed potential benefits of DPS are unknown.

7. There is (a) lack of familiarity with many aspects of DPS; and (b) insufficient information exchange among regulators, policymakers, and power sector entities.

8. The states should lead on DPS policymaking, although the federal government should have a role in setting a foundational energy policy framework.

9. Combined heat and power (CHP) and storage are DPS applications with large untapped potential.

10. In order to realize the full benefits of DPS, policies need to be "smarter": differentiating by technology stage of development and project size.

Many of these policies, predominantly aimed at increasing the penetration of renewable energy sources, are viewed by stakeholders as effective at increasing DPS penetration. However, some policies, particularly at the state level, are viewed by stakeholders as lacking clarity regarding their interaction with other polices or incentives. Stakeholders see a clear requirement for DPS-related policies that provide a greater degree of consistency and predictability. CHP and storage are DPS applications identified by respondents as holding large untapped potential, and therefore as particularly good candidates for more targeted policy support.

DPS may have a positive impact on reliability and security of electricity delivery in the civilian sector. DPS can decrease vulnerability by allowing the 'islanding' of military installations and bases from the grid when necessary. DPS technologies can also be used to improve the efficiency—and therefore reduce the vulnerability—of forces in the combat theater.

6.2 Recommendations

Based on the economic and policy analysis and the outreach to stakeholders conducted for this study, we conclude that increased penetration of DPS has the potential to make a significant positive contribution to the U.S. power system. The principal benefits of DPS are their ability to contribute a new resource to the U.S. power supply portfolio thereby diversifying the nation's power supply options, to relieve grid congestion and decrease transmission and distribution line losses, to avoid the construction of some new utility-scale power plants, to capture the value of currently under-utilized resources, and to utilize some of the new capabilities of a modern grid such as the two-way flow of power. The value of DPS is enhanced by their potential ability to realize environmental and reliability-related benefits without the need for agreements on the siting and financing of large capacity and transmission additions to the electric grid.

The extent to which DPS can realize their potential depends in part on the ability to quantify the full range of costs and benefits of greater penetration including the potential cost of carbon emissions. The authors therefore advocate a series of policies that allow the benefits of DPS to be quantified, evaluated, and realized relative to other power supply resources.

In general, we support policies that provide information, transparency, and choice on prices and technologies in a way that captures the economic, environmental, and energy security benefits of DPS in an affordable way.

DPS policymaking should adhere to the following principles:[1]

- Provide technology choices and price transparency
- Limit impact on ratepayers; if costs to support DPS are above market, decrease them over time
- Limit the amount of government subsidies; decrease them over time as the market matures
- Leverage private sector investment
- Remain technology neutral

Within these guidelines, there are discrete roles for federal and state governments. Many of the policy tools, approaches, and concepts outlined here draw on the considerable work that other organizations and individuals have done, especially in assessing lessons learned and developing best practice guidelines. Our goal is to highlight the policies we think best create a "level playing field" for DPS, while addressing the concerns and views of the industry stakeholders outlined in previous chapters.

Federal Government

There are a wide variety of DPS-related policy tools available at the federal, state, and local levels. These tools would function better under a foundational policy that sets clear objectives. Respondents in our outreach mostly agreed that some combination of overarching, comprehensive federal energy-climate legislation would provide the kind of certainty and predictability that investors need. Federal government policy-makers need to establish policies that are durable enough to match the business planning cycle of investors, developers, utilities, and other companies in the power sector.[2]

The federal government has a role to play in establishing policy directions; harmonizing regulations; supporting research, development, and demonstration; and leading by example as a major provider and consumer of energy. The federal government should act as a "convener" to bring parties together at all levels on policy direction and to set minimum or broadly applicable national standards and regulations. The federal government should also use public power as an example-setter, and use those parts of the system the government controls—including the military—to develop and demonstrate major policies and practices.

We recommend the following specific, federal policy approaches that could fulfill this mandate:

1. Adopt a Carbon Pricing Policy   The majority of respondents interviewed and surveyed for this study said that the introduction of a price on carbon would greatly assist in the energy planning process in general and in the development and deployment of DPS specifically. The federal government should take the lead in setting a national carbon pricing mechanism that accounts for the real economic externalities of carbon dioxide emissions. A price on carbon should take the form of either a carbon tax, where carbon emissions are subject to a per-unit tax on carbon emitted; or through the implementation of a cap-and-trade system, through which a ceiling is established for the maximum amount of carbon emissions permitted in the economy, with industries and sectors required to comply with predetermined carbon limits or pay to exceed them. While opinions among those surveyed and members of the research team varied, some members of the research team expressed a significant preference for a carbon tax as they feel a carbon tax system is more difficult to game than a cap-and-trade system. These members of the research team expressed particular support for a revenue-neutral carbon tax such as the one implemented in British Columbia. Given the inability to reach a workable economy-wide carbon tax or cap-and-trade system in Congress, a more moderate approach of a regionally differentiated carbon tax on the electricity sector could provide significant impact at relatively low cost. Under this approach, power plant emissions would be taxed at a regional rate that provides similar rate impacts in all regions, for example 2 percent. This mitigates the heavy impact on the Midwest and South by having a lower carbon tax in these regions.[3]

Absent a carbon pricing mechanism, a final, albeit indirect, means of pricing carbon emissions is through the implementation of a "clean energy standard" (CES), which mandates a minimum percentage of power generation from sources that qualify as "clean" with penalties for non-compliance. A CES is less effective than a carbon tax or a cap-and-trade system for assigning a carbon price owing to its focus on generation rather than on emissions, and to the challenge of defining what qualifies under the standard.

2. Support Clean Energy Innovation and Expand Sustained Research and Development Funding   Government support for R&D is a critically important means for spurring innovation and moving new energy technologies into the market. As noted, many DPS technologies have benefited from a rapid decrease in unit costs in recent years with some now approaching cost-competitiveness with central power generation. Expanded technology R&D is likely to improve the performance of DPS.

One potential mechanism to achieve the requisite levels of R&D is the establishment of a Clean Energy Development Authority (CEDA). The *Clean Energy Financing Act of 2011* sponsored by Chairman Jeff Bingaman (D-NM) and Sen. Lisa Murkowski (R-AK) of the Senate Energy and Natural Resources Committee would create such an entity to finance the development and deployment of advanced energy technologies. CEDA would focus on ensuring adequate financing throughout the life-cycle of an innovative technology.

In addition, the set of recommendations recently issued by the American Energy Innovation Council (AEIC) should be seriously considered:[4]

- *Create an independent national Energy Strategy Board:* Charged with developing and monitoring a national energy plan for Congress and the executive branch, as well as "guiding and coordinating energy research investments by DOE, CEDA and the New Energy Challenge Program" (see below).[5]
- *Invest $16 billion per year in clean energy innovation:* Including basic energy science, renewables, fossil energy, efficiency, and other areas.
- *Create Centers of Excellence with strong domain expertise:* Building on the Department of Energy's Energy Innovation Hubs, these centers would be located at universities and national labs to concentrate and leverage resources.
- *Fund ARPA-E at $1 billion per year:* ARPA-E (Advanced Research Projects Agency—Energy), created with a mission "to fund projects that will develop transformational technologies . . . in the ways we generate, store, and utilize energy," requires continued government support.[6] The AEIC points out, however, that ARPA-E could only fund

one percent of the proposals it received in its first year of operation.[7] ARPA-E's initial budget was $400 million, and its current FY 2012 request is for $650 millon.[8]

- *Establish and fund a New Energy Challenge Program to build large-scale pilot projects:* Under an independent corporation outside of the federal government and in partnership with private industry, the program would "focus on the transition from pre-commercial, large-scale energy systems to integrated, full-size systems."[9]

3. Extend Existing Federal Legislation for Renewable Energy
In an effort to better target financial support for renewable energy, reduce government outlays, and leverage private sector support, the federal government should extend the term and financing of the Section 1603 cash grant program.

Section 1603 of the ARRA allows project developers to receive cash payments in lieu of investment tax credits and allows those eligible for a production tax credit (PTC) to receive an investment tax credit (ITC) or equivalent cash grant. It was implemented to simplify the tax credit process and to provide greater access to financing for renewable energy projects. The program, which is set to expire at the end of 2011, has been successful: $9.2 billion has been spent funding nearly 20,000 projects across the country, supporting 13.6 GW of capacity and 35 TWh of electricity generation.[10] A recent analysis by the Bipartisan Policy Center (BPC) indicates that using cash grants is more effective than—and half as expensive as—the tax equity approach.[11]

We recommend the extension of the Section 1603 program. In addition, we endorse the BPC's recommendations that tax credits be implemented for a period of at least five years to provide the predictability that investors need; that the federal government consider providing a production-based cash grant; and that the government study the costs and potential benefits of allowing Master Limited Partnerships for renewable energy entities.[12]

4. Promote Education and Information-Sharing   The federal government can play a leading role in promoting greater awareness of DPS, including education and information-sharing programs. For example, the U.S. DOE supports eight Clean Energy Application Centers around the country, with a mandate "to promote CHP, waste heat recovery, and other clean energy technologies and practices and offer regional assistance for specific projects throughout the United States," through market assessments, targeted education and outreach, and technical assistance.[13] DOE could consider the feasibility of expanding the efforts of the centers, or alternatively examine the establishment of similar institutional efforts for non-CHP technologies and applications.

An excellent example of expanding information sharing and partnering approaches is the Electric Power Research Institute's (EPRI) Smart Grid Demonstration Initiative, a seven year effort started in 2008. One goal of the initiative is to "share the best information and lessons learned on integrating distributed energy resources and specific technical issues of various distribution systems."[14]

In the area of information-sharing and capacity-building for state utility regulators, the U.S. DOE funds several key efforts. The ARRA provided $44 million to state commissions for hiring and training of staff, and in March of 2010 DOE established a cooperative agreement with the National Association of Regulatory Utility Commissioners (NARUC) for "provision of capacity assistance and consultant expertise to States, the development of new training programs, and sharing of information and best practices among States on ARRA-related issues."[15] These resources are managed under NARUC's State Electricity Regulators Capacity Assistance and Training (SERCAT) program, and in 2010 seven awards were issued addressing such issues as developing aggregated net metering for renewable resources in Arizona and evaluating smart grid reliability benefits in Illinois. This type of support needs to be expanded in order to ensure that the knowledge base of state regulators keeps pace with the objectives and requirements of rapidly changing state policies, as well as the dynamics of the market.

5. **Conduct Research on DPS Impacts on Reliability and Security**   The increased deployment of DPS is likely to have implications for the reliability and security of the U.S. power system. Public and private sector stakeholders tackling the challenge of upgrading the grid to minimize vulnerability and costs from outages need information on the reliability-related costs and benefits of DPS. We recommend that the federal government conduct a thorough assessment of the reliability-related costs and benefits of DPS. EPRI has identified several areas for further research and information-sharing that directly address issues raised in our stakeholder outreach, and could also form the basis for this federal support. These include: (a) comprehensive study of distributed energy resources including storage, incorporating the smart grid, in a central vs. distributed generation paradigm; (b) accelerate development and deployment of high efficiency technology options; (c) accelerate plug and play features of distributed generation appliances, and; (d) conduct pilot deployment to demonstrate costs and benefits to the grid and society.[16] We endorse these as targeted, top-tier priorities.

The adoption of DPS is also likely to have an impact on the vulnerability of the grid to cyber-attack. As the number of generation source- and smart grid-related technologies

The Solyndra Effect

Many DPS projects benefit from government support, which comes in various forms (investment tax-credits, grants, and loan guarantees to name a few). Some initial government support is often critical in creating a more level playing field for emerging technologies by helping less commercialized technologies to achieve cost reductions through economies of scale. At the time of writing, loan guarantees for energy projects were under particular scrutiny following the bankruptcy of Solyndra, a solar cell manufacturer that received roughly $535 million in government loan guarantees.[17] Although loan guarantees merely indicate that the government is required to cover the costs of a loan if the borrower defaults on its payment obligations (and often the government can recoup some of the costs through the seizure of company assets), the immediate political furor surrounding Solyndra suggests that future government loan guarantees will encounter far greater scrutiny. Indeed soon after the bankruptcy of Solyndra, SolarCity announced that it would have to scale back the scope of its SolarStrong project, as it was unable to secure a loan guarantee from DOE.[18]

Despite the rising criticism of federal loan guarantees in the wake of Solyndra's bankruptcy, evidence suggests that such guarantees can be an effective means of stimulating private sector investment and promoting key renewable energy technologies.[19] Some members of our research team feel that the federal government should consider the continued selected use of loan guarantee programs in areas such as early-stage research and development. Other members of the research team, pointing to the example of Solyndra, and also the more recent example of electric car maker Fisker Automotive, which likewise appears to have benefitted substantially from federal loans while failing to deliver on key promised benefits, believe that such programs create inherent and fundamental problems that outweigh any potential advantages.

proliferate, there are concerns that the grid will be more vulnerable to attack through more points of entry. There has been much work done on the cybersecurity impact of the smart grid, notably by the National Institute of Standards and Technology (NIST)'s Cyber Security Working Group (CSWG) of the Smart Grid Interoperability Panel. We recommend that the federal government adopt the CSWG's guidelines into legislation to the extent practicable.

6. Use Federal Government to Help Demonstrate and Commercialize DPS   The federal government is a large user of energy, and thus is in a unique position to play a role in demonstrating and deploying DPS. For example, the White House estimates that the federal government occupies nearly 500,000 buildings and buys $500 billion annually in goods and services.[20] On October 9, 2009, the president signed Executive Order 13423 establishing various energy objectives for federal government entities, such as Greenhouse Gas Management and Sustainable Buildings and Communities.[21] The order requires government agencies to develop a Strategic Sustainability Performance Plan, including goals for "increasing agency use of renewable energy and implementing renewable energy generation projects on agency property," and "aligning federal policies to increase the effectiveness of local planning for energy choices such as locally generated renewable energy."[22] These efforts should continue to be implemented, monitored and evaluated, and expanded where necessary. In addition, the *Blueprint for a Secure Energy Future* announced by the White House in March 2011 described ongoing federal efforts and initiatives going forward.

7. Support DPS through Military Procurement and deployment   The United States military has a compelling incentive to adopt DPS, which can help it meet its renewable energy and energy-efficiency goals; improve the security of power delivery to bases at home and abroad; and provide advantages for expeditionary activities in theater.

The energy-security and operational benefits of military DPS are frequently calculated on an ad hoc and unsystematic basis. Through continued development of appropriate methodologies, the military can better assess the true value of DPS projects. We recommend that the U.S. military develop a more formal scheme for systematizing and quantifying DPS risks and benefits. Such a scheme should include a means of allowing the armed forces to accurately internalize the fully-burdened cost of fuel for expeditionary energy on the battlefield as recommended by Defense Science Board in 2001 and 2008.

The United States has more than one thousand bases and military installations in sixty-three countries.[23] These bases are often connected in various ways to power infrastructures with varying reliability. As it looks to maximize the reliability and security of its operating environments both in the United States and overseas, the U.S. military should consider distributed generation and microgrids as an essential part of its electricity generation strategy.

Through large-scale procurement, the military can help to drive down the unit costs of renewable DPS technologies, and serve as a pioneer for other sectors of the economy looking to move down the learning curve on issues including installation, operation, and maintenance of DPS. For expeditionary operations, we recommend that the military expand programs such as the Rucksack Enhanced Portable Power System (REPPS) that use DPS technologies to reduce the use of liquid fuels on the front lines and increase the efficiency of personnel in theater.

For expeditionary military activity we recommend a strategy of continuing to develop and deploy promising DPS technologies with a focus on those technologies that will be most vital to enhancing the core fighting effectiveness of these expeditionary forces. In discussions with military leaders directly involved in energy issues, they repeatedly stressed that those technologies most likely to succeed would be those focused on improving the mission, from which some of the other possible benefits of DPS (such as increased reliability, environmental friendliness, or even lower cost) are ultimately only side benefits.

State Governments

States have been the primary "policy-lab" for DPS to date and should continue to play the central role in developing DPS policies through state governments, legislatures, utility regulatory commissions, and local entities. Since DPS are designed and implemented closest to customers at the distribution level, barriers and solutions are more location-specific, and state and local institutions are best equipped to address them. However, state and local policies do not operate in a vacuum and, as described above, federal policy plays a key role in setting national priorities and broad direction.

Given the number of renewable or alternative energy portfolio standards in place in states across the United States, it appears that the goal for many states is to reduce carbon emissions as well as to reap the benefits of a green economy including job creation, energy security, and cleaner air. The specific renewable or alternative energy goals of each state may vary, the standards may have a wide range, and the qualifying energy sources may vary, but these states clearly have an environmental goal to reduce carbon emissions.

The Need for Differentiated DPS Policies

DPS projects can range from very small projects to much larger projects. These different project sizes require different investment amounts and varying amounts of risk, and they require a different policy response. In addition, there is a fundamental difference between providing power for self-supply (a retail transaction) and selling power to the utility for resale to end-use customers (a wholesale transaction).

Given the nature of retail and wholesale electricity markets in the United States today, we recommend that policy tools for DPS be differentiated according to the size and type of project. Net metering (with some kind of dynamic pricing mechanism) is the most appropriate policy tool for self-supply DPS projects, while production-based policies—either in the form of FITs or set through an auction—are the most appropriate policy tool for medium-sized DPS projects that sell their power into the wholesale market for resale. For large DPS projects (those over 100 MW, for example), we believe that the most appropriate state policy tool is the renewable portfolio (or alternative energy) standard.

In Table 6.1, we provide a matrix of policy mechanisms most appropriate for each project size and type of sale.

Below are some specific recommendations for each project size.

Small Projects

1. Allow Net Metering for Small DPS Projects   Most states currently allow small DPS projects for self-supply (those up to around 2 MW) to be net-metered. This approach should be adopted by all states to allow DPS to compete with other resources in the power sector.

2. Implement a DPS Dynamic Pricing Mechanism for Accurately Valuing Customer-sited DPS Generation   Accurately pricing customer-sited DPS is fundamental to the future

TABLE 6.1 POLICY OPTIONS FOR DIFFERENT DPS PROJECT SIZES

Policy Option	Project Size			# of States		Type of Sale
	Small (< 2 MW)	Medium (2 to 100 MW)	Large (> 100 MW)	Adopted	Under Review	
Net Metering	X			45 States & DC		Retail
Feed-In Tariff		X		5	4	Wholesale
Reverse Auction Market		X		CA		Wholesale
Renewable Portfolio Standard			X	29 States & DC		Wholesale

of DPS as a resource in the U.S. power system. Currently, self-generated power is supplied at the retail rate (i.e., the meter runs backwards) and most excess customer-generated power credited at the customer's retail rate. To more accurately reflect the value of the power produced, states should consider pricing DPS using a dynamic rate. This rate could be the average spot market price for the excess power generated; the real-time price, the locational marginal price, or a critical peak price. Pricing the power produced by DPS using a dynamic rate can help eliminate the need to limit the amount of DPS on a system. However, if DPS are not priced accurately, there can be an oversupply of DPS in places on the system where power is not needed. Customers on DPS systems should not remain on flat rates.

    3. Do Not Set Capacity Limits by DPS Power Source Just as DPS should be allowed to compete with other generation sources, states should not use quotas or upper limits to discriminate among different DPS sources. While this may result in an environment that disadvantages more expensive technologies, the latter can be supported by financial incentives.

4. Apply Common Net Metering Models and Interconnection Standards   Net metering policies currently vary in terms of eligible renewable energy sources, limits on system capacity for each project, limits on aggregate capacity (as a percent of a utility's peak demand), how net excess generation is handled, and whether meter aggregation is permitted. To provide clarity to DPS investors and operators, net metering terms should be harmonized to apply consistently to all utilities within a state. To the same end, state PUCs and energy commissions should work to implement common interconnection standards.

Medium-sized projects

5. Design Feed-In Tariffs that Place an Initial Cap on Capacity; Phase Out the Cap Over Time as FIT Prices Ratchet Down to Competitive Prices   A major challenge in using FITs as an incentive mechanism for DPS is the difficulty of setting appropriate prices. States that want to use FITs to increase the amount of DPS on a system should consider designing FITs that set a cap for capacity that phases out over time as FIT prices ratchet down to competitive prices. Such an approach will increase the competitiveness of DPS technologies and applications, while reducing the impact of this resource on ratepayers.

6. Use Reverse Auctions as a Method for Promoting DPS   Rather than setting a predetermined price for a FIT to incentivize DPS development, states should consider the use of reverse auctions through which the tariff rate is set by bids from eligible DPS developers. Such auctions provide a market-based mechanism for setting price levels and thereby limit the impact of this resource on ratepayers. In our view, auctions are the preferred mechanism for pricing DPS.

Large Projects

7. Allow DPS to be Eligible for RPS Without Discrimination States with renewable portfolio standards in place should include power generated by renewable DPS as eligible for meeting the goal without limits or quotas.

Recommendations for Further Study

In addition to the recommendations above, there are a number of policy approaches that were raised by stakeholders in our outreach whose adoption may enable the potential value of DPS to be realized. States should consider a full evaluation of these policy approaches as they seek to maximize the economic and environmental potential of all resources at their disposal.

1. Decoupling or Lost Revenue Recovery within the Current Regulatory Framework   Much of the feedback from stakeholders about the potential and appropriate role for DPS addressed the question of the future structure and business model of the U.S. power sector. For those who want to see a paradigm shift in the way that power is sold and consumed, decoupling is an essential mechanism for incentivizing efficiency and promoting competition from non-utility generators. As stated in Chapter 4, thirteen states have decoupling mechanisms in place with another nine pending, and nine states have lost revenue recovery mechanisms in place with two pending.[24] A full evaluation of the merits of decoupling is beyond the scope of this paper. However, it is clear that widespread adoption of decoupling or some type of lost revenue recovery mechanism would have potentially beneficial results for DPS.

2. Promotion of Community and Aggregated Systems Establishing policies and regulations that permit aggregated DPS and microgrids can provide multiplier benefits for local communities and utilities. Specific mechanisms include virtual net metering, energy improvement districts, and community choice aggregators.[25]

3. Collection and Dissemination of Distribution System Information Requiring utilities to assess, map, and publish technical information on the distribution system can greatly facilitate the siting of DPS. A CPUC decision required PG&E, SCE, and SDGE, to "provide the 'available capacity' at the substation or circuit level in map format."[26] It goes on to say, "If unable to initially provide this level of detail each IOU must provide the data at the most detailed level feasible, and work to increase the precision of the information over time." In Minnesota, the Next Generation Energy Act of 2007 required a statewide study to look into how much distributed generation could contribute into its renewable energy portfolio and what locations would be best for distributed generation projects.[27]

4. Incorporation of DPS into Planning (Prudence Reviews) In a budget-constrained environment along with high energy prices, a good low-cost fall-back approach is to consider all technologies in resource planning. Utilities need a broader menu of choices and should be free to pursue any technology that makes sense. This has worked at the federal level and needs to carry over to the state level. This would be supported by uniform cost effectiveness tests (see below) and local integrated resource planning that targets marginal distribution costs.

5. Development of Cost Effectiveness Criteria There are standard cost effectiveness tests used by PUCs, which typically apply to energy efficiency and take into account all of the costs and benefits of such systems as well as the winners and losers. Similar tools could be required to quantify and monetize the benefits of DPS.

6. **Establishment of Peak Demand Reduction Standards** This mechanism refers to programs requiring utilities to reduce peak demand by a specific amount. For example, in 2009, the Ohio Public Utilities Commission developed rules for energy efficiency and demand reduction benchmarks such that "each electric utility is required to implement peak-demand reduction programs designed to achieve established statutory benchmarks for peak-demand reduction."[28] California, in its Assembly Bill 2021 of 2006, also required the California Energy Commission and the California Public Utilities Commission to develop efficiency savings and demand reduction targets for ten years.[29] Although peak-demand reduction goals would benefit DPS, such goals could in fact result in an oversupply of DPS at a price above market. We believe that a market mechanism such as demand reduction in response to a market price signal (i.e., demand response or DR) is a more appropriate and cost-effective mechanism for meeting peak demand reduction goals. Since the potential for DR is quite large in the United States, we believe that DR should be the "go to" mechanism for reducing peak demand rather than demand reduction mandates.

7. **Third-Party Ownership** One recent approach to alleviate the burden of high up-front capital costs of renewable energy projects for individuals and small institutions has been for third parties to install, own, and operate all equipment and facilities, and then provide the power to the customer. However, in some states, third-party distributed generation owners may be considered electricity providers and thus subject to regulatory

commission oversight. States should consider instituting the necessary statutory changes to allow third-party ownership of DPS to avoid the increased costs and administrative requirements associated with regulated-entity status.

State and Federal Support for Key DPS Applications

Given the large potential benefits that could be captured from CHP and storage, we recommend that both federal and state governments establish a more robust policy framework to support these applications. While we are not endorsing particular previously proposed legislation, we highlight several mechanisms below that should be considered by policymakers.

Storage

The Electricity Storage Association (ESA) supports a number of policies for energy storage to be competitive as an energy resource such as incorporation of storage in the prudence reviews for utility resource planning, investment tax credits and loan guarantees, set-asides in portfolio standards, and federal R&D funding. Specific federal policies include:

- **The Clean Energy Financing Act of 2011:** Creating CEDA (described in Section 6.2.1).
- **S.1351, or the Battery Innovation Act:** To promote development, manufacturing and use of advanced batteries, Senator Debbie Stabenow (D-MI) referred the Battery Innovation Act to the Senate Committee on Energy and Natural Resources. It is the first coordinated plan to include all aspects of advanced battery production such as R&D, raw material availability, and manufacturing.

The bill also seeks to create an Energy Innovation Hub to bring together universities, businesses and nonprofits in the development of these technologies.

- **Storage Technology of Renewable and Green Energy Act of 2009 (STORAGE):** Senator Ron Wyden (D-OR) proposed this bill that would provide a 20 percent investment tax credit for various types of energy storage facilities and equipment, and another tax credit that would apply to electrical storage technologies that connect to electricity transmission and distribution systems. A 30 percent tax credit in the bill is provided for onsite use in individual homes, businesses, and factories. There is also financing for smart grid devices to manage the charging and storage of electricity. Home and factory owners could use the tax credits to finance individual thermal cooling systems or biomass equipment installation and steam power. The tax credit is based on the amount of energy stored and not on the type of technology.[30]

- **State Initiatives:** At the state level, the California Energy Storage Alliance supports California's AB 2514 requiring "CPUC, by March 1, 2012, to open a proceeding to determine appropriate targets, if any, for each load-serving entity to procure viable and cost-effective energy storage systems and, by October 1, 2013, to adopt an energy storage system procurement target, if determined to be appropriate, to be achieved by each loadserving entity by December 31, 2015, and a second target to be achieved by December 31, 2020." Similar requirements are made of the governing board of local publicly-owned electric utilities. The CPUC has already initiated proceedings, requesting and receiving comments from industry stakeholders. Storage is also included in California's SGIP.

CHP

It is clear from our modeling and feedback from the participants in our research, as well as a wide range of recent, supporting studies, that there are considerable untapped benefits from CHP.[31] CHP advocates support several basic policy initiatives to realize this potential, including output-based emissions rules for all generators, inclusion of CHP in any portfolio standards or standard offer programs, financial incentives, and enhanced awareness and education. Some specific policy efforts to be considered include the Clean Local Energy Efficiency and Renewables Act of 2011 (CLEER), with provisions for an investment tax credit of 10 percent for CHP and tax exempt bonds for the financing of certain energy plants and; Texas Law HB 1831 (2009) requires any organization that is building or making major renovations to a critical government facility to undertake first a CHP feasibility study and directs that "when the expected energy savings of the CHP system exceed the expected costs of purchasing, operating, and maintaining the system over a 20-year period, equipping the facility with a combined heating and power system is preferred to promote energy security."[32]

ANNEX 1:
COST-BENEFIT ANALYSIS
MODEL ASSUMPTIONS

TABLE 1A.1 DG ASSUMPTIONS IN THE HIGH COST SCENARIO

	Fuel Cell (Electric Only) Biogas	Fuel Cell (Electric Only)	Fuel Cell CHP	Fuel Cell CHP (Biogas)	Solar PV Roof <10kW	Solar PV Roof Commercial 100–500kW
System Performance	(Solar PV capacity factors and costs expressed on a DC basis)					
System Size (MW)	0.1	0.1	0.4	0.4	0.01	0.25
System Lifetime (Years)	20	20	20	20	25	25
Annual Capacity Factor (DC for PV)	72.0%	72.0%	72.0%	72.0%	16.5%	17.5%
Degradation Factor (%/yr)	1.0%	1.0%	1.0%	1.0%	1.25%	1.25%
System Cost						
Capital Cost ($/kW)	$13,319	$10,569	$7,995	$10,745	$6,599	$5,800
Interconnection ($/kW)						
Construction and Development ($/kW)						
Owner's Cost ($/kW)						
Total System Cost ($/kW)	$13,319	$10,569	$7,995	$10,745	$6,599	$5,800
Debt Service Reserve Fund (True/False)	TRUE	TRUE	TRUE	TRUE	TRUE	TRUE
Fuel Costs						
Fuel Type	Biogas	Gas	Gas	Biogas	None	None
Fuel Cost ($/MMBtu)	$10.00	$5.95	$5.95	$10.00	$0.00	$0.00
Fuel Cost Escalation	2.5%	2.5%	2.5%	2.5%		
Heat Rate (Btu/kWh)	7,418	7,418	8,282	8,282		
Ongoing Costs						
Fixed O&M Cost–Regional ($/kW-yr)	$0.00	$0.00	$0.00	$0.00	$30.00	$30.00
Fixed O&M Cost–Escalator (%/yr)	2.0%	2.0%	2.0%	2.0%	2.0%	2.0%
Variable O&M Cost ($/MWh)	$40.00	$20.00	$35.00	$54.00		
Variable O&M Cost–Escalator (%/yr)	2.5%	2.5%	2.5%	2.5%		
Insurance Expense ($/kW-yr)					$26	$23
Insurance Escalator (%/yr)					2.0%	2.0%
Inverter Replacement Cost ($/W)					$0.37	$0.32
Inverter Replacement Time (Years)					10	10
Royalty Payment to Landowner (% of gross earnings)						
Financing Assumptions						
% Financed with Equity (Output if DSCR Constrained = TRUE)	50%	54%	56%	56%	58%	58%
After-Tax WACC	8.25%	8.25%	8.25%	8.25%	8.25%	8.25%
Debt Interest Rate	7.50%	7.50%	7.50%	7.50%	7.50%	7.50%
Cost of Equity	12.10%	11.44%	11.30%	11.30%	10.97%	10.97%
Debt Period in Years	20	20	20	20	20	20
DSCR Constrained	TRUE	TRUE	TRUE	TRUE	TRUE	TRUE
DSCR Target	1.40	1.40	1.40	1.40	1.40	1.40
Minimum % Equity if DSCR Constrain is TRUE	20%	20%	20%	20%	20%	20%
Income Tax Assumptions						
Income Tax–Federal	35%	35%	35%	35%	35%	35%
Income Tax–State	8.84%	8.84%	8.84%	8.84%	8.84%	8.84%
Income Tax–Effective Rate	40.75%	40.75%	40.75%	40.75%	40.75%	40.75%
Income Tax–MACRS Term	5	5	5	5	5	5
Federal Tax Credit Assumptions						
Federal Tax Credit–ITC (%)	30%	30%	30%	30%	30%	30%
Federal Tax Credit–% Capital Cost Eligible for ITC	95%	95%	95%	95%	100%	100%
Maximum ITC $/kW	$3,000	$3,000	$3,000	$3,000	$10,000	$10,000
Federal Tax Credit–PTC ($/MWh)	$0	$0	$0	$0		
Federal Tax Credit–PTC (Years)	0	0	0	0		
Federal Tax Credit–PTC Escalation (%)	2.5%	2.5%	2.5%	2.5%		
Levelized Busbar Costs						
Busbar Cost ($/MWh)	$307	$198	$191	$286	$385	$321
System + Finance Costs	$268	$210	$158	$213	$548	$454
O&M Costs	$130	$73	$97	$156	$50	$45
Property Tax	$0	$0	$0	$0	$0	$0
Income Tax–State	($9)	($8)	($6)	($7)	($22)	($18)
Tax Credit–State	$0	$0	$0	$0	$0	$0
Income Tax–Federal	($21)	($19)	($14)	($18)	($56)	($46)
Tax Credit–Federal	($61)	($59)	($44)	($58)	($159)	($132)
Debt Service Coverage Ratio (DSCR)	1.40	1.40	1.40	1.40	1.40	1.40

Solar PV 2–5MW Ground/ Fixed-Tilt	Solar PV 5–20MW Ground/ Fixed-Tilt	Gas Turbine CHP	Gas Turbine CHP (Biogas)	Microturbine CHP	Microturbine CHP Biogas	IC Engine CHP	IC Engine CHP Biogas	Wind 2–5MW	Wind Samll Community (300–500kW)
5	20	1	1	0.165	0.165	0.8	0.8	5	0.387
25	25	20	20	20	20	20	20	20	20
18%	19.5%	72.0%	72.0%	72.0%	72.0%	72.0%	72.0%	25.0%	18.0%
1.0%	1.0%	1.0%	1.0%	1.0%	1.0%	1.0%	1.0%	1.0%	1.0%
$4,397	$3,927	$2,582	$5,332	$3,622	$6,372	$2,554	$5,304	$2,907	$3,406
$4,397	$3,927	$2,582	$5,332	$3,622	$6,372	$2,554	$5,304	$2,907	$3,406
TRUE	TRUE	TRUE	TRUE	TRUE	TRUE	TRUE	TRUE	TRUE	TRUE
None	None	Gas	Biogas	Gas	Biogas	Gas	Biogas	None	None
$0.00	$0.00	$5.95	$10.00	$5.95	$10.00	$5.95	$10.00	$0.00	$0.00
		2.5%	2.5%	2.5%	2.5%	2.5%	2.5%		
		11,766	11,766	13,540	13,540	9,749	9,749		
$20.00	$32.00	$0.00	$0.00	$0.00	$0.00	$0.00	$0.00		
2.0%	0.0%	0.0%	0.0%	0.0%	0.0%	0.0%	0.0%		
		$20.00	$54.00	$20.00	$86.00	$20.00	$54.00	$8.00	$8.00
		2.5%	2.5%	2.5%	2.5%	2.5%	2.5%	2.5%	2.5%
$18									
2.0%									
$0.25									
10									
55%	55%	45%	45%	37%	37%	44%	44%	42%	38%
8.25%	8.25%	8.25%	8.25%	8.25%	8.25%	8.25%	8.25%	8.25%	8.25%
7.50%	7.50%	7.50%	7.50%	7.50%	7.50%	7.50%	7.50%	7.50%	7.50%
11.33%	11.36%	12.94%	12.94%	14.73%	14.68%	13.07%	13.04%	13.53%	14.46%
20	20	20	20	20	20	20	20	20	20
TRUE	TRUE	TRUE	TRUE	TRUE	TRUE	TRUE	TRUE	TRUE	TRUE
1.40	1.40	1.40	1.40	1.40	1.40	1.40	1.40	1.40	1.40
20%	20%	20%	20%	20%	20%	20%	20%	20%	20%
35%	35%	35%	35%	35%	35%	35%	35%	35%	35%
8.84%	8.84%	8.84%	8.84%	8.84%	8.84%	8.84%	8.84%	8.84%	8.84%
40.75%	40.75%	40.75%	40.75%	40.75%	40.75%	40.75%	40.75%	40.75%	40.75%
5	5	5	5	5	5	5	5	5	5
30%	30%	10%	10%	30%	30%	10%	10%		
95%	95%	95%	95%	95%	95%	95%	95%		
$10,000	$10,000	$10,000	$10,000	$200	$200	$10,000	$10,000		
								$21	$21
								10	10
								2.5%	2.5%
$243	$184	$143	$281	$178	$371	$129	$258	$136	$225
$333	$274	$53	$108	$75	$133	$52	$108	$176	$283
$30	$20	$101	$194	$112	$250	$88	$172	$9	$9
$0	$0	$0	$0	$0	$0	$0	$0	$0	$0
($12)	($10)	($1)	($3)	($2)	($3)	($1)	($3)	($7)	($10)
$0	$0	$0	$0	$0	$0	$0	$0	$0	$0
($29)	($24)	($4)	($8)	($3)	($4)	($4)	($8)	($24)	($37)
($93)	($77)	($5)	($11)	($5)	($5)	($5)	($11)	($19)	($19)
1.40	1.40	1.40	1.40	1.40	1.40	1.40	1.40	1.40	1.40

TABLE 1A.2 DG ASSUMPTIONS IN THE LOW COST SCENARIO

	Fuel Cell (Electric Only) Biogas	Fuel Cell (Electric Only)	Fuel Cell CHP	Fuel Cell CHP (Biogas)	Solar PV Roof <10kW	Solar PV Roof Commercial 100–500kW
System Performance	(Solar PV capacity factors and costs expressed on a DC basis)					
System Size (MW)	0.1	0.1	0.4	0.4	0.01	0.25
System Lifetime (Years)	20	20	20	20	25	25
Annual Capacity Factor (DC for PV)	85.0%	85.0%	85.0%	85.0%	17.9%	19.5%
Degradation Factor (%/yr)	1.0%	1.0%	1.0%	1.0%	1.0%	1.0%
System Cost						
Capital Cost ($/kW)	$10,897	$8,647	$6,541	$8,791	$5,399	$4,950
Interconnection ($/kW)						
Construction and Development ($/kW)						
Owner's Cost ($/kW)						
Total System Cost ($/kW)	$10,897	$8,647	$6,541	$8,791	$5,399	$4,950
Debt Service Reserve Fund (True/False)	TRUE	TRUE	TRUE	TRUE	TRUE	TRUE
Fuel Costs						
Fuel Type	Biogas	Gas	Gas	Biogas	None	None
Fuel Cost ($/MMBtu)	$10.00	$5.95	$5.95	$10.00	$0.00	$0.00
Fuel Cost Escalation	2.5%	2.5%	2.5%	2.5%		
Heat Rate (Btu/kWh)	7,418	7,418	8,282	8,282		
Ongoing Costs						
Fixed O&M Cost–Regional ($/kW-yr)	$0.00	$0.00	$0.00	$0.00	$30.00	$30.00
Fixed O&M Cost–Escalator (%/yr)	2.0%	2.0%	2.0%	2.0%	2.0%	2.0%
Variable O&M Cost ($/MWh)	$40.00	$20.00	$35.00	$54.00		
Variable O&M Cost–Escalator (%/yr)	2.5%	2.5%	2.5%	2.5%		
Insurance Expense ($/kW-yr)					$27.00	$22.00
Insurance Escalator (%/yr)					2.0%	2.0%
Inverter Replacement Cost ($/W)					$0.37	$0.32
Inverter Replacement Time (Years)					12.5	12.5
Royalty Payment to Landowner (% of gross earnings)						
Financing Assumptions						
% Financed with Equity (Output if DSCR Constrained = TRUE)	55%	55%	57%	57%	58%	58%
After-Tax WACC	8.25%	8.25%	8.25%	8.25%	8.25%	8.25%
Debt Interest Rate	7.50%	7.50%	7.50%	7.50%	7.50%	7.50%
Cost of Equity	11.38%	11.36%	11.18%	11.10%	10.96%	10.96%
Debt Period in Years	20	20	20	20	20	20
DSCR Constrained	TRUE	TRUE	TRUE	TRUE	TRUE	TRUE
DSCR Target	1.40	1.40	1.40	1.40	1.40	1.40
Minimum % Equity if DSCR Constrain is TRUE	20%	20%	20%	20%	20%	20%
Income Tax Assumptions						
Income Tax–Federal	35%	35%	35%	35%	35%	35%
Income Tax–State	8.84%	8.84%	8.84%	8.84%	8.84%	8.84%
Income Tax–Effective Rate	40.75%	40.75%	40.75%	40.75%	40.75%	40.75%
Income Tax–MACRS Term	5	5	5	5	5	5
Federal Tax Credit Assumptions						
Federal Tax Credit–ITC (%)	30%	30%	30%	30%	30%	30%
Federal Tax Credit–% Capital Cost Eligible for ITC	95%	95%	95%	95%	100%	100%
Maximum ITC $/kW	$3,000	$3,000	$3,000	$3,000	$10,000	$10,000
Federal Tax Credit–PTC ($/MWh)	$0	$0	$0	$0		
Federal Tax Credit–PTC (Years)	0	0	0	0		
Federal Tax Credit–PTC Escalation (%)	2.5%	2.5%	2.5%	2.5%		
Levelized Busbar Costs						
Busbar Cost ($/MWh)	$242	$159	$163	$246	$287	$242
System + Finance Costs	$183	$145	$109	$147	$405	$342
O&M Costs	$130	$73	$97	$157	$46	$39
Property Tax	$0	$0	$0	$0	$0	$0
Income Tax–State	($6)	($5)	($4)	($5)	($16)	($14)
Tax Credit–State	$0	$0	$0	$0	$0	$0
Income Tax–Federal	($15)	($13)	($9)	($12)	($41)	($35)
Tax Credit–Federal	($49)	($41)	($30)	($41)	($118)	($99)
Debt Service Coverage Ratio (DSCR)	1.40	1.40	1.40	1.40	1.40	1.40

Solar PV 2–5MW Ground/ Fixed-Tilt	Solar PV 5–20MW Ground/ Fixed-Tilt	Gas Turbine CHP	Gas Turbine CHP (Biogas)	Microturbine CHP	Microturbine CHP Biogas	IC Engine CHP	IC Engine CHP Biogas	Wind 2–5MW	Wind Samll Community (300–500kW)
5	20	1	1	0.165	0.165	0.8	0.8	5	0.387
25	25	20	20	20	20	20	20	20	20
20.0%	21.3%	85.0%	85.0%	85.0%	85.0%	85.0%	85.0%	36.0%	32.0%
1.0%	1.0%	1.0%	1.0%	1.0%	1.0%	1.0%	1.0%	1.0%	1.0%
$3,510	$3,000	$2,112	$4,362	$2,964	$5,214	$2,090	$4,340	$2,430	$2,786
$3,510	$3,000	$2,112	$4,362	$2,964	$5,214	$2,090	$4,340	$2,430	$2,786
TRUE	TRUE	TRUE	TRUE	TRUE	TRUE	TRUE	TRUE	TRUE	TRUE
None	None	Gas	Biogas	Gas	Biogas	Gas	Biogas	None	None
$0.00	$0.00	$5.95	$10.00	$5.95	$10.00	$5.95	$10.00	$0.00	$0.00
		3%	3%	3%	3%	3%	3%		
		11,766	11,766	13,540	13,540	9,749	9,749		
$20.00	$32.00	$0.00	$0.00	$0.00	$0.00	$0.00	$0.00		
2.0%	0.0%	0.0%	0.0%	0.0%	0.0%	0.0%	0.0%		
		$20.00	$54.00	$20.00	$86.00	$20.00	$54.00	$8.00	$8.00
		2.5%	2.5%	2.5%	2.5%	2.5%	2.5%	2.5%	2.5%
$15.00	$0.00								
2.0%	0.0%								
25%	0.0%								
12.5	0.0								
56%	55%	48%	48%	31%	41%	47%	47%	32%	32%
8.25%	8.25%	8.25%	8.25%	0.0%	8.25%	8.25%	8.25%	8.25%	8.25%
7.50%	7.50%	7.50%	7.50%	0.0%	7.50%	7.50%	7.50%	7.50%	7.50%
11.29%	11.36%	12.42%	12.42%	0.0%	13.73%	12.69%	12.56%	16.30%	16.37%
20	20	20	20	20	20	20	20	20	20
TRUE	TRUE	TRUE	TRUE	TRUE	TRUE	TRUE	TRUE	TRUE	TRUE
1.40	1.40	1.40	1.40	1.40	1.40	1.40	1.40	1.40	1.40
20%	20%	20%	20%	20%	20%	20%	20%	20%	20%
35%	35%	35%	35%	35%	35%	35%	35%	35%	35%
8.84%	8.84%	8.84%	8.84%	8.84%	8.84%	8.84%	8.84%	8.84%	8.84%
40.75%	40.75%	40.75%	40.75%	40.75%	40.75%	40.75%	40.75%	40.75%	40.75%
5	5	5	5	5	5	5	5	5	5
30%	30%	10%	10%	30%	30%	10%	10%	0.0%	0.0%
95%	95%	95%	95%	95%	95%	95%	95%	0.0%	0.0%
$10,000	$10,000	$10,000	$10,000	$200	$200	$10,000	$10,000		
								$0	$0
								10	10
								2.5%	2.5%
$176	$133	$131	$256	$142	$335	$117	$233	$95	$119
$239	$192	$36	$75	$22	$91	$36	$74	$103	$132
$26	$18	$101	$194	$120	$251	$88	$172	$9	$9
$0	$0	$0	$0	$0	$0	$0	$0	$0	$0
($8)	($7)	($1)	($1)	$0	($1)	($1)	($2)	($4)	($5)
$0	$0	$0	$0	$0	$0	$0	$0	$0	$0
($20)	($17)	($2)	($4)	$1	($1)	($2)	($5)	($14)	($18)
($67)	($54)	($3)	($7)	($1)	($4)	($3)	($7)	$0	$0
1.40	1.40	1.40	1.40	1.40	1.40	1.40	1.40	1.40	1.40

ANNEX 2:
STAKEHOLDER SURVEY

Definition: For the purposes of this survey, Distributed Power Systems are defined as "electric generation systems that supply power at distribution-level voltages or lower, whether on the utility side of the meter, or on the customer side; and distribution-level electricity storage applications."

1. How would you characterize the potential of distributed power systems (DPS) to meet the following aspects of the nation's energy-related priorities?

Economic

High	☐
Medium	☐
Low	☐
Unsure	☐

Environmental

High	☐
Medium	☐
Low	☐
Unsure	☐

Energy security
 High ☐
 Medium ☐
 Low ☐
 Unsure ☐

2. What do you see as being the top three principal benefits of DPS? (check three)
 Cost savings in production and delivery of power ☐
 Increased system reliability ☐
 Improved power quality ☐
 Reduced land-use effects ☐
 Reduced vulnerability of the power system ☐
 Reduced environmental impacts ☐
 Do not see any benefits of DPS ☐
 Other—please specify below ☐
 Answer here: _____

3. Do you think more should be done by policymakers and/or regulators to promote greater penetration of DPS?
 Yes ☐
 No ☐

4. If you answered "yes" to question 3, who do you think should have primary responsibility for doing more to promote DPS?
 Federal Energy Regulatory Commission ☐
 Environmental Protection Agency ☐
 Department of Energy ☐
 State governments ☐
 Public utility commissions ☐
 Municipal/local authorities ☐

5. **What do you see as the top three policy barriers to greater penetration of DPS?**

   Interconnection requirements and costs ☐

   Rate-related impediments[1] ☐

   Federal/state regulatory jurisdictional issues ☐

   Lack of financing mechanisms ☐

   Environmental siting and permitting requirements ☐

   Concerns over safety and reliability ☐

   Lack of information about the benefits of DPS ☐

   Other—please specify below ☐

   Answer here: ─────────────────────

6. **How effective do you think the adoption of the following policy mechanisms would be in addressing the above challenges and increasing penetration of DPS?**

   a) **A price on CO_2 (carbon tax, cap-and-trade system)**

   Very effective ☐

   Somewhat effective ☐

   Not very effective ☐

   Not at all effective ☐

   Unsure ☐

   b) **National Renewable Portfolio Standard**

   Very effective ☐

   Somewhat effective ☐

   Not very effective ☐

   Not at all effective ☐

   Unsure ☐

   c) **National Clean Energy Portfolio Standard**

   Very effective ☐

   Somewhat effective ☐

   Not very effective ☐

   Not at all effective ☐

   Unsure ☐

d) State-level Renewable Portfolio Standard
Very effective ☐
Somewhat effective ☐
Not very effective ☐
Not at all effective ☐
Unsure ☐

e) Creation of Wholesale Markets for Power Produced through Distributed Generation
Very effective ☐
Somewhat effective ☐
Not very effective ☐
Not at all effective ☐
Unsure ☐

f) Adoption of Uniform Interconnection Standards
Very effective ☐
Somewhat effective ☐
Not very effective ☐
Not at all effective ☐
Unsure ☐

g) Feed-In Tariff
Very effective ☐
Somewhat effective ☐
Not very effective ☐
Not at all effective ☐
Unsure ☐

h) Tax Incentives for Purchase and Installation
Very effective ☐
Somewhat effective ☐
Not very effective ☐
Not at all effective ☐
Unsure ☐

7. In your view, how effective are the amendments to PURPA of the Energy Policy Act of 2005 and the Energy Independence and Security Act of 2007 (the so-called "must-consider" standards) in advancing the adoption of DPS?

   Very effective ☐
   Somewhat effective ☐
   Not very effective ☐
   Not at all effective ☐
   Unsure ☐

8. Which of the following measures have the most potential to overcome the rate-related impediments to distributed generation? (check two)

   Dynamic (time-based) electricity pricing ☐
   Net metering ☐
   Smart metering ☐
   Demand response programs ☐
   None of the above ☐
   Unsure ☐

9. Aside from the policy measures outlined above, what more should the federal, state or local governments do to encourage the adoption of DPS?

   Federal government

   State government

   Local government

10. **How would you categorize your organization?**

Investor-owned utility ☐

Public-owned/municipal utility ☐

Utility cooperative ☐

Federal utility ☐

Non-utility Qualifying Facility/IPP ☐

Regulator ☐

Consumer group ☐

Other ☐

NOTES

Introduction

1. Non-hydro new summer renewable energy capacity from 1989 to 2009 increased by approximately 312 percent (U.S. Energy Information Administration, *Annual Energy Review 2009*), Washington, DC: U.S. Government Printing Office, 264.
2. For an in-depth review of this issue, see C. Ebinger and K. Massy "Software and Hard Targets: Enhancing Smart Grid Cybersecurity in the Age of Information Warfare," research paper, Brookings Institution, Washington, DC, February 2011.

Chapter 1

1. "The Changing Structure of the Electric Power Industry 2000: An Update," Office of Coal, Nuclear, Electric and Alternate Fuels, U.S. Energy Information Administration, U.S. Department of Energy, Washington, DC: U.S. Government Printing Office, October 2000, 114.
2. Richard Hirsch, *Technology and Transformation in the American Electric Utility Industry* (Cambridge, UK: Cambridge University Press, 2003).
3. Eric Martinot, Ryan Wiser, and Jan Hamrin, "Renewable Energy Policies and Markets in the United States," Center for Resource

Solutions (2005) (http://www.efchina.org/csepupfiles/report
/2007122104842884.369074320503.pdf/RE_Policies&Markets_US.pdf).

4. Ibid.

5. "PURPA, A Mixed Blessing," part of "FERC Notices of Proposed
   Rulemaking on Electricity," Federal Energy Regulatory Commission
   (FERC), March 29, 1988.

6. Severin Borenstein and James Bushnell, "Electricity Restructuring:
   Deregulation or Reregulation?" *Regulation* 23, (2), Cato Institute, 2000.
   An interesting parallel can be drawn with the situation in 2011 as
   unexpectedly low natural gas prices increase the challenge to the
   economics of renewable power generation.

7. "Construction Costs for New Power Plants Continue to Escalate
   IHS-CERA Power Capital Costs Index," IHS CERA press release,
   May 27, 2008 (http://energy.ihs.com/News/Press-Releases/2008
   /IHS-CERA-Power-Capital-Costs-Index.htm).

8. Vikram S. Budhraja, Fred Mobasheri, Margaret Cheng, Jim Dyer,
   Eduyng Castano and Stephen Hess, "California's Electricity
   Generation and Transmission Interconnection Needs Under Alternative Scenarios: Assessment of Resources, Demand, Need for Transmission Interconnections, Policy Issues and Recommendations for Long
   Term Transmission Planning," (Prepared for California Energy
   Commission) Electric Power Group, LLC, November 17, 2003
   (http://www.electricpowergroup.com/Downloads
   /pFinalCAElecGenTransNeeds11-17T3.pdf).

9. Thomas Ackermann, Goran Andersson, and Lennart Soder,
   "Distributed generation: a definition," *Electric Power Systems
   Research* 57 (2001): 195–204 (http://paginas.fe.up.pt/~cdm/DE2
   /DG_definition.pdf).

10. P. Dondi, D. Bayoumi, C. Haederli, D Julian, and M. Suter, "Network
    integration of distributed power generation," *Journal of Power Sources*
    106 (2002): 1–9.

11. "Accommodating High Levels of Variable Generation," North
    American Electric Reliability Corporation (NERC) Special
    Report (April 2009): 60 (http://www.nerc.com/files/IVGTF_Report
    _041609.pdf).

12. Energy Policy Act of 2005 (EPAct), Section 917.

13. N. Hatziargyriou, "Modeling New Forms of Generation and Storage," CIGRE Technical Brochure, TF 38.01.10 (Paris: CIGRE, November 2000.)

14. Many definitions of distributed energy include demand response and end-user efficiency. While the authors recognize the value of these resources and the large potential they have for improving the performance and reliability of the power system, they were not included in the definition of DPS owing to a desire to focus on the relative competitiveness of generation technologies and a limited capacity to undertake a detailed analysis of end-user behavioral economics.

15. "The Potential Benefits of Distributed Generation and Rate-Related Issues That May Impede Their Expansion: A Study Pursuant to Section 1817 of the Energy Policy Act of 2005," U.S. Department of Energy, February 2007 (http://www.ferc.gov/legal/fed-sta /exp-study.pdf).

16. Vaclav Smil, "Energy at the Crossroads" (Background notes for presentation at the Global Science Forum Conference on Scientific Challenges for Energy Research, Paris, May 17–18, 2006); "BP Statistical Review of World Energy," June 2011 (http://www.bp.com/assets/bp _internet/globalbp/globalbp_uk_english/reports_and_publications /statistical_energy_review_2011/STAGING/local_assets/pdf/statistical _review_of_world_energy_full_report_2011.pdf). Calculations: World energy consumption in 2010 = 12,000; MTOE = 511; EJ = 142,070 TWh; Solar insolation has a global mean of 170 W/m2 = 122,000 TW.

17. Rhead Enion, "2010 U.S. Solar Market: $6 billion," *Legal Planet: The Environmental Law and Policy Blog*, March 10, 2011 (http://legalplanet .wordpress.com/2011/03/10/2010-u-s-solar-market-6-billion).

18. See the Solar Energy Industries Association website (http://www .seia.org).

19. Included in this total were 2,086 MW of photovoltaics (PV) and 507 MW of utility-scale concentrating solar power.

20. "2010 U.S. Wind Industry Annual Market Report: Rankings," American Wind Energy Association (AWEA), Updated May 2011

(http://www.awea.org/learnabout/publications/factsheets/upload
/2010-Annual-Market-Report-Rankings-Fact-Sheet-May-2011.pdf).

21. *Electric Power Annual 2009*, U.S. Energy information Administration,
U.S. Department of Energy (http://www.eia.gov/cneaf/electricity/epa
/epa_sprdshts.html); and "U.S. Wind Industry Year-End 2010 Market
Report," American Wind Energy Association, January 2011.

22. "2009 Wind Technologies Market Report," U.S. DOE Energy Efficiency
& Renewable Energy, August 2010 (http://www1.eere.energy.gov
/windandhydro/pdfs/2009_wind_technologies_market_report.pdf).

23. See FloDesign Wind Turbine (www.fdwt.com).

24. "AWEA Small Wind Turbine Global Market Study," American Wind
Energy Association, 2010.

25. "Form EIA-861 Data for 2008," U.S. Energy Information Administration
(http://www.eia.doe.gov/cneaf/electricity/page/eia861.html). Units that
are 10MW or less.

26. Esteve Juanola-Feliu, "Nanobiotechnologies: Technology transfer and
commercialization emerging from science and technology parks for
green growth in Spain" (Presentation, Daejon, Korea, May 24, 2010).

27. "Diesel and Gas Generator Market—Global Market Size, Equipment
Market Share and Competitive Landscape Analysis to 2020," GlobalData
report, December 2010.

28. "Backup Generators (BUGS): The Next Smart Grid Peak Resource,"
National Energy Technology Laboratory, April 2010.

29. "Clean Heat & Power Basics," United States Clean Heat & Power
Association (http://www.uschpa.org/i4a/pages/index
.cfm?pageid=3283).

30. Ibid.

31. Anna Shipley et al, "Combined Heat and Power: Effective Energy Solutions for a Sustainable Future," Oak Ridge National Laboratory, 2008.

32. "Co-generation and Renewables: solutions for a low-carbon energy
future," International Energy Agency, May 2011.

33. "Hydropower Report," ABS Energy Research, 2009.

34. Alison M. Conner, James E. Francfort, and Ben N. Rinehart, "U.S.
Hydropower Resource Assessment Final Report" (prepared for
U.S. DOE), Idaho National Engineering and Environmental Laboratory,
Renewable Energy Products Department, Lockheed Martin Idaho

Technologies Company, December 1998 (http://hydropower.inel.gov
/resourceassessment/pdfs/doeid-10430.pdf).

35. A.B.G. Thilak, "Global Small Hydro Power Market Analysis to 2020—
Installed Capacity, Generation, Investment Trends," GlobalData (http://
www.altenergymag.com/emagazine.php?art_id=1532).

36. "Fuel Cell Industry is Poised for Major Change and Development in
2011," Pike Research, February 2, 2011 (http://www.pikeresearch.com
/newsroom/fuel-cell-industry-is-poised-for-major-change-and
-development-in-2011); "Global Fuel Cell Market by Technology,
Application, Component, Installation, Cost, Geography, Trends
and Forecasts (2011–2016)," marketsandmarkets.com, May 2011
(http://www.marketsandmarkets.com/Market-Reports
/fuel-cell-market-348.html).

37. "The World Market for Microgrids," SBI Energy report, February 2011.

38. B.H. Puttengen, R.P. MacGregor, and C.F. Lambert, "Distributed
generation: Semantic hype to the dawn of a new era?" *IEEE Power and
Energy Magazine* 1:1 (Jan/Feb 2003): 22–29 (http://ieeexplore.ieee.org
/xpl/freeabs_all.jsp?arnumber=1180357).

39. Ibid.

40. "The Potential Benefits of Distributed Generation and Rate-Related
Issues That May Impede Their Expansion: A Study Persuant to
Section 1817 of the Energy Policy Act of 2005," U.S. Department of
Energy (February 2007) 1–7 (http://www.ferc.gov/legal/fed-sta
/exp-study.pdf).

41. Larry Sherwood, "U.S. Solar Market Trends," Interstate Renewable
Energy Council (IREC), (June 2011): 6.

42. Andrew Herndon, "NRG Gets U.S. Guarantee for $2.6 Billion Rooftop
Solar Plan," *Bloomberg*, June 22, 2011 (http://www.bloomberg.com
/news/2011-06-22/u-s-offers-guarantee-for-2-6-billion-nrg-rooftop
-solar-program.html).

43. "SolarCity to Install on Military Homes, Doubling Residential Solar,"
Los Angeles Times, September 7, 2011 (http://latimesblogs.latimes
.com/money_co/2011/09/solarcity-to-install-solar-on-military-homes
-doubling-residential-solar.html).

44. Anne Chittum and Nate Kauffman, "Challenges Facing Combined Heat
and Power Today: A State-by-State Assessment," American Council for

an Energy-Efficient Economy Report No. IE111, May 2011, 2 (Chittum and Kauffman, 2011).

45. R. Neal Elliott and Mark Spurr, "Combined Heat and Power: Capturing Wasted Energy," American Council for an Energy-Efficient Economy Research Report No. IE983, May 1, 1999.

46. Ibid.

47. Chittum and Kauffman, 2011.

48. "Promoting Biomass CHP Projects in Northwestern U.S.," *Cogeneration & On-Site Power Production*, January 3, 2011 (http://www.cospp.com /articles/print/volume-12/issue-2/features/promoting-biomass-chp -projects-in-northwestern-us.html).

49. "Microturbines Eligible for California's Self Generation Incentive Program (SGIP)," *The Wall Street Journal MarketWatch*, September 20, 2011 (http://www.marketwatch.com/story/microturbines-eligible-for -californias-self-generation-incentive-program-sgip-2011-09-20).

50. "Nellis activates nation's largest PV array," U.S. Air Force Nellis Air Force Base, December 19, 2007 (http://www.nellis.af.mil/news/story .asp?id=123079933).

51. "Information on the Navy's Geothermal Program," GAO-04-513, United States Government Accountability Office, June 2004.

52. "GE to Transform U.S. Military Base into Smart Grid Showcase," GE press release, July 8, 2009 (http://www.ge-ip.com/news-events /detail/2592).

53. Cheryl Pellerin, "DOD Gives High Priority to Saving Energy," *American Forces Press Service*, United States Department of Defense, September 29, 2011 (http://www.defense.gov/news/newsarticle .aspx?id=65480).

Chapter 2

1. The notable exception for the last thirty or forty years has been larger-scale distributed combined heat and power (CHP) which provides higher efficiency than central station generation and is a mainstay of large industrial facilities, particularly in oil and gas.

2. E3's levelized cost analysis is fully documented and publicly available. The analysis can be verified and updated using E3's Distributed Energy Costing Model available at www.ethree.com.

3. "SGIP Staff Proposal and Workshops," California Public Utilities Commission, last modified: February 15, 2011 (http://www.cpuc .ca.gov/PUC/energy/DistGen/sgip/proposal_workshops.htm); "California Solar Initiative Cost-Effectiveness Evaluation," E3 (Prepared for the California Public Utilities Commission), April 2011 (http:// ethree.com/documents/CSI/CSI percent20Report_Complete_E3 _Final.pdf); "Tools & Spreadsheets," California Public Utilities Commission, last modified: June 17, 2011 (http://www.cpuc.ca.gov /PUC/energy/Procurement/LTPP/LTPP2010/2010+LTPP+Tools+and +Spreadsheets.htm).

4. "LTPP Solar PV Performance and Cost Estimates: Potential and Levelized Cost of Energy (LCOE)," E3, June 18, 2010 (http://www .ethree.com/documents/LTPP/LTPP percent20Presentation.pdf).

5. The costs of central station generation are based on E3's work for the Western Electricity Coordinating Council. The spreadsheet and assumptions are available at www.wecc.biz in the TEPPC committee area under documents, and "E3 Costing Tool." The low values for transmission and distribution capacity value are zero, and the high values are $40/kW-year and $100/kW-year respectively and converted to $/MWh assuming a 50 percent distributed generation capacity factor. Natural gas is the relevant comparison for much of the West and Northeast, and coal-fired steam turbines (which) reflect the predominant generation type in the Midwest, South, and Southeast.

6. The capital costs, capacity factors, heat rates, operation and maintenance costs, financing, and taxes were taken from ITRON's recent report on natural-gas-fueled distributed generation and wind projects. The assumptions for PV systems were taken from the CSI Cost-Effectiveness Report and the CPUC procurement analysis.

Chapter 3

1. "ENERGY STAR Data Center Energy Efficiency Initiatives." (http://www .energystar.gov/index.cfm?c=prod_development.server_efficiency).

2. "Keeping the Lights On in a New World," Electricity Advisory Committee Report to U.S. Department of Energy, January 2009 (http:// energy.gov/sites/prod/files/oeprod/DocumentsandMedia/adequacy _report_01-09-09.pdf).

3. Adapted from: "Electrical Reliability," Powervar: Solutions for Power Quality (http://www.powervar.com/electrical-reliability.cfm).

4. Galvin Electricity Initiative, "The Electric Power System is Unreliable" (http://www.galvinpower.org/resources/library/fact-sheets-faqs /electric-power-system-unreliable).

5. K. Hamachi-La Commare and E. Joseph Eto, "Understanding the Cost of Power Interruptions to the U.S. Electricity Consumers," September 2004.

6. However, given the significantly higher number of commercial sector customers (14.9 million) compared to industrial customers (1.6 million), the industrial sector's cost per outage per customer is significantly higher than those of the commercial customers.

7. Timothy J. Brennan, "Electricity Markets and Energy Security: Friends or Foes?" *Resources*, Fall/Winter 2008 (http://www.rff.org /Publications/Resources/Pages/ElectricityMarkets.aspx).

8. Arthur D. Little, Inc., "Reliability and Distributed Generation," 2000.

9. Edison Electric Institute, "Underground vs. Overhead Distribution Wires: Issues to Consider," May 2000.

10. Alexander E. Farrell, Lester B. Lave, and Granger Morgan, "Bolstering the Security of the Electric Power System," *Issues in Science and Technology* Spring 2002 (http://www.issues.org /18.3/farrell.html).

11. "A Survey of Transmission Cost Allocation Issues, Methods and Practices," PJM, March 10, 2010 (http://ftp.pjm.com/~/media /documents/reports/20100310-transmission-allocation-cost -web.ashx).

12. John DiStassio, Statement to the House Subcommittee on Energy and Environment, Protecting the Electirc Grid: H.R. 2165, the Bulk Power System Protection Act of 2009, and H.R. 2195, October 27, 2009.

13. The Internet is enabled by the Transmission Control Protocol and the Internet Protocol (together, TCP/IP) which enable communication between programs on different computers and applications such as the World Wide Web, remote admistration, file transfer, and email.

14. Franklin D. Kramer, Stuart H. Starr, and Larry Wentz, *Cyberpower and National Security* (Washington, DC: National Defense University Press, 2009).

15. Robert Lemos, "'Data Storm' Blamed for Nuclear-Plant Shutdown," *SecurityFocus*, May 18, 2007. (http://www.securityfocus.com /news/11465).

16. "From Barracks to Battlefield: Clean Energy Innovation and America's Armed Forces," The Pew Project on National Security, Energy and Climate, September 21, 2011 (http://www.pewenvironment.org /news-room/reports/from-barracks-to-battlefield-clean-energy -innovation-and-americas-armed-forces-85899364060).

17. Ibid.

18. "More Fight—Less Fuel," Office of the Under Secretary of Defense For Acquisition, Technology, and Logistics, U.S. Department of Defense, February 2008 (Department of Defense, February 2008).

19. Ibid.

20. Mayumi Negishi and James Topham, "Japan Tells Arms Supplier to Probe Cyber Attack," *Reuters*, September 20, 2011 (http:// www.reuters.com/article/2011/09/20/us-mitsubishi-heavy -idUSTRE78J1N320110920); William J. Broad, John Markoff, and David Sanger, "Israeli Test on Worm Called Crucial in Iran Nuclear Delay," *The New York Times*, January 15, 2011.

21. CIA World Factbook, Country Comparison Oil Consumption. Accessed at https://www.cia.gov/library/publications/the-world -factbook/rankorder/2174rank.html

22. "From Barracks to Battlefield: Clean Energy Innovation and America's Armed Forces," The Pew Project on National Security, Energy and Climate, September 21, 2011.

23. "Casualty Costs of Fuel and Water Resupply Convoys in Afghanistan and Iraq," *Army-Technology*, February 26, 2010 (http://www.army -technology.com/features/feature77200).

24. Roxana Tiron, "$400 per Gallon Gas to Drive Debate over Cost of War in Afghanistan," The Hill, October 15, 2009.

25. John M. McHugh, "August 10, 2011—Secretary of the Army remarks at GovEnergy Conference, Cincinnati, Ohio," U.S. Army, September 1, 2011 (http://www.army.mil/article/64731).

26. Department of Defense, February 2008.

27. "Energy for the Warfighter: Operational Energy Strategy," U.S. Department of Defense, 2008.

28. Department of Defense, February 2008.

29. Ibid.

30. Many military bases have or are in the process of privatizing electric assets and infrastructure. Accordingly, implementation of DPS independent grid operation for system security may need to coordinate with electric utility initiatives or as an adjunct system that would operate independently from the electric utility grid.

31. "From Barracks to Battlefield: Clean Energy Innovation and America's Armed Forces," The Pew Project on National Security, Energy and Climate, September 21, 2011 (http://www.pewenvironment.org /news-room/reports/from-barracks-to-battlefield-clean-energy -innovationand-americas-armed-forces-85899364060).

32. Notably, microgrid application for military bases now has the attention of U.S. congressional representatives. In May, 2010, the Military Energy Security Act (MESA) was submitted under The National Defense Authorization Act for Fiscal Year 2011 (H.R. 5136). The bill passed the House but was not approved for 2012—it may be reintroduced in subsequent sessions. MESA, as proposed, included $25 million for a microgrid "pilot program" that would be implemented at a military base by 2014 (Representative Martin Heinrich (D-NM) sponsored the bill).

33. Adam Seawall, "Size of U.S. Solar PV Home Systems Growing, IREC Industry Report Says," getsolar.com, 30 June 2011 (http://www.getsolar .com/blog/size-of-u-s-solar-home-pv-systems-growing-irec -industry-report-says/18107).

34. "From Barracks to Battlefield: Clean Energy Innovation and America's Armed Forces," The Pew Project on National Security, Energy and Climate, September 21, 2011 (http://www.pewenvironment.org /news-room/reports/from-barracks-to-battlefield-clean-energy -innovation-and-americas-armed-forces-85899364060).

35. "Solar Power Sources: Rucksack Enhanced Portable Power System," U.S. Army RDECOM, CERDEC Army Power Division (http://www .cerdec.army.mil/directorates/docs/c2d/REPPS_Fact_Sheet.pdf) and Tony Bui, "New Army Battery Recharging Kits Run on Renewable Energy," *Armed with Science*, August 24, 2010 (http://science.dodlive .mil/2010/08/24/new-army-battery-recharging-kits-run-on -renewableenergy).

Chapter 4

1. These include: the Database of State Incentives for Renewables and Efficiency (DSIRE), funded by the U.S. Department of Energy and maintained by the N.C. Solar Center and the Interstate Renewable Energy Council (IREC) (http://dsireusa.org); the American Council for an Energy-Efficient Economy (ACEEE) (http://www.aceee.org /node/2958/all); the Center for Climate and Energy Solutions (http:// www.c2es.org/us-states-regions); IREC (http://irecusa.org); the National Governors Association (http://www.nga.org/cms/home /nga-center-for-best-practices/center-publications/page-eet -publications/col2-content/main-content-list/clean-and-secure -state-energy-ac.html); and the Clean Energy States Alliance (http:// www.cleanenergystates.org).

2. Some readers will no doubt call attention to other policies that are not mentioned in our analysis that are applicable in some way to DPS. However, to focus the analysis, the research team decided to highlight those we judged to be the most illustrative and relevant, while recognizing that the entire panoply of policy tools and their interrelationships are part of the policy framework.

3. See the DSIRE website at www.dsireusa.org for more details on rules and regulations surrounding implementation.

4. Ibid.

5. "1703," U.S. Department of Energy Loan Programs Office (https://lpo.energy.gov/?page_id=39)

6. "1705," U.S. Department of Energy Loan Programs Office (https://lpo.energy.gov/?page_id=41).

7. "Our Mission," U.S. Department of Energy Loan Programs Office (https://lpo.energy.gov/?page_id=17). On September 30, 2011, the Loan Guarantee Program's Section 1705 expired.

8. "Our Projects," U.S. Department of Energy Loan Programs Office (https://lpo.energy.gov/?page_id=45). Includes $10.647 billion in loans under Section 1703 and $16.0265 billion under Section 1705.

9. MACRS was created in 1986 and updated in the EPAct 2005 and again under the Energy Improvement and Extension Act of 2008.

10. The bonus depreciation was introduced in the Economic Stimulus Act of 2008 and continued in 2009 and 2010 through the ARRA 2009 and Small Business Jobs Act, respectively. It was expanded in the Tax Relief, Unemployment Insurance Reauthorization and Job Creation Act of 2010 to include a 100 percent first year bonus depreciation for systems purchased and installed between September 8, 2010 and the end of 2011. See www.dsireusa.org for more specific rules and regulations governing this program.

11. See: "Subtitle E—Amendments to PURPA of the Energy Policy Act of 2005: Sections 1251a, §11, and 1254a, §15."

12. R. Brent Alderfer, Thomas J. Starrs, and M. Monika Eldridge, "Making Connections: Case Studies of Interconnection Barriers and their Impact on Distributed Power Projects," National Renewable Energy Laboratory NREL/SR-200-28053, May 2000 (revised July 2000).

13. See: "Order No. 2006. Standardization of Small Generator Interconnection Agreements and Procedures," Federal Energy Regulatory Commission, issued May 12, 2005.

14. Ibid.

15. See: *MidAmerican*, 94 FERC ¶ 61, 340 (2001). From "FERC Upholds Net Metering Laws," *Wind Energy Weekly*, 20,940 (April 6, 2001).

16. See: *MidAmerican*, 94 FERC ¶ 61,340 (2001), and *SunEdison LLC*, 129 FERC ¶ 61, 146 (2009).

17. See: Section 1252 of EPAct 2005; and New PURPA Section 210(m) "Regulations Applicable to Small Power Production and Cogeneration Facilities," Federal Energy Regulatory Commission, January 2006.

18. New PURPA Section 210(m) "Regulations Applicable to Small Power Production and Cogeneration Facilities," Federal Energy Regulatory Commission, January 2006.

19. "130 FERC ¶ 61, 214: Revisions to Form, Procedures, and Criteria for Certification of Qualifying Facility Status for a Small Power Production or Cogeneration Facility," Federal Energy Regulatory Commission Order No. 732 and Docket No. RM09-23-000, issued March 19, 2010.

20. California Public Utilities Commission, 133 FERC 61,059, 2010.

21. Frederick A. Fucci, "Distributed Generation," in *The Law of Clean Energy*, ed. Michael B. Gerard (Chicago: American Bar Association, 2011), 345–358.

22. Ibid.

23. "Notice of Inquiry 135 FERC ¶ 61,240," Federal Energy Regulatory Commission, June 2011. Quotation from "FERC Seeks Comment on Policies for Ancillary Services, Electric Storage Technologies," Federal Energy Regulatory Commission News, June 16, 2011.

24. "Smart Grid," DOE Office of Electricity Delivery & Energy Reliability (http//energy.gov/oe/technology-development/smart-grid).

25. "TITLE XIII, SEC. 1301 (3)," Energy Independence and Security Act of 2007.

26. See: "NIST Priority Action Plan 07 6.2.3." (http://www.nist.gov/smartgrid/upload/7-Energy_Storage_Interconnection.pdf). Also see Priority Action Plan 09 section 6.2.1, on Standard DR and DER Signals, which announced its objectives to define a framework and common terminology for demand energy resource integration (http://www.nist.gov/smartgrid/upload/9-Standard_DR_signals.pdf).

27. See: "Section 1141" of the American Recovery and Reinvestment Act of 2009.

28. See: "Title IV Subtitle D—Energy Storage for Transportation and Electric Power," also known as the United States Energy Storage Competitiveness Act of 2007.

29. We do not examine sources of financing for states. For an excellent summary of approaches in this area, see Devashree Saha, Sue Gander, and Greg Dierkers, "State Clean Energy: Financing Guidebook," National Governors Association, January 2011. For updated details on specific state programs and design features, please refer to the Database of State Incentives for Renewables and Efficiency (DSIRE) online (http://www.dsireusa.org).

30. Charles Kubert and Mark Sinclair, "Distributed Renewable Energy Finance and Policy Toolkit," Clean Energy States Alliance, December 2009 (CESA 2009).

31. Ibid.

32. Ibid.

33. Ibid.

34. Ibid.

35. Ibid.

36. Charles Kubert and Mark Sinclair, "A Review of Emerging State Finance Tools to Advance Solar Generation," Clean Energy States Alliance, March 2010 (CESA 2010).

37. "Feed-in Tariffs (FIT): Frequently Asked Questions for State Utility Commissions," National Association of Regulatory Utility Commissioners (NARUC), June 2010 (NARUC 2010). FITs are established in the states of California, Hawaii, Vermont, Maine, and Oregon, as well as in the cities of Sacramento, CA, San Antonio, TX, Madison, WI, and Gainesville, FL, and by the utility Consumer's Energy in Michigan; they have been proposed in Indiana, Ohio, Washington, Wisconsin, Michigan, Minnesota, and Rhode Island.

38. CESA 2010.

39. NARUC 2010.

40. "DSIRE: Summary Tables," http://dsireusa.org/summarytables/index.cfm?ee=1&RE=1.

41. "Compare State Policies," http://www.aceee.org/node/124.

42. Julie Taylor, "Feed-in Tariffs (FIT): Frequently Asked Questions for State Utility Commissions," The National Association of Regulatory Utility Commissioners, June 2010.

43. Ibid.

44. For an in-depth review of this issue, see Scott Hempling, Carolyn Elefant, Karlynn Cory, and Kevin Porter, "Renewable Energy Prices in State-Level Feed-in Tariffs: Federal Law Constraints and Possible Solutions," NREL Technical Report NREL/TP-6A2-47408, January 2010.

45. "FERC clarifies California feed-in tariff procedures," Federal Energy Regulatory Commission (FERC) News Release, October 21, 2010 (http://www.ferc.gov/media/news-releases/2010/2010-4/10-21-10-E-2.asp).

46. Ryan Wiser, "State of the States: Update on RPS Policies and Progress," Lawrence Berkeley National Laboratory (presentation at the Renewable Energy Markets 2010, Portland, Oregon, October 20, 2010) (LBNL 2010).

47. According to the Pew Center on Global Climate Change, Massachusetts has flywheel energy storage in its alternative energy portfolio

standard. See: http://www.pewclimate.org/docUploads/State-RPS
-percent20Detail.pdf and http://www.pewclimate.org/what_s_being
_done/in_the_states/rps.cfm.

48. See: "Net Metering Model Rules," Interstate Renewable Energy
Council, 2009.

49. Laurel Varnado and Michael Sheehan, "Connecting to the Grid,"
Interstate Renewable Energy Council, 2009 (sixth edition), 13–17
(IREC 2009a).

50. NREL 2000.

51. See IREC 2009a, p. 18 for background on the evolution and development
of these procedures and differences.

52. "State Electric Efficiency Regulatory Frameworks," Institute for Electric Efficiency, June 2011 (http://www.edisonfoundation.net/IEE
/issueBriefs/IEE_StateRegulatoryFrame_0611.pdf).

53. "Output-Based Regulations," U.S. EPA Combined Heat and Power
Partnership (http://www.epa.gov/chp/state-policy/output.html).

54. "Output-Based Emissions Regulations," American Council for an
Energy-Efficient Economy (http://www.aceee.org/sector/state-policy
/toolkit/chp/emissions).

55. "Output-Based Regulations: A Handbook for Air Regulators,"
U.S. Environmental Protection Agency, August 2004 (http://
www.epa.gov/chp/documents/obr_final_9105.pdf).

56. See: "Output-Based Emissions Standards for Distributed Generation,"
Regulatory Assistance Project Issues Letter, July 2003 (RAP 2003).

57. Ibid.

58. Ibid.

59. Neeharika Naik-Dhungel, "Output-Based Regulations: Best Practices Option for CHP," U.S. Environmental Protection Agency
Combined Heat and Power Partnership, July 13, 2011 (http://www
.intermountaincleanenergy.org/events/2011-07-13/Output-Based
_Regulations.pdf).

60. "Plug-in Electric Vehicles," The PEW Center of Global Climate
Change. Updated: August 10, 2011 (http://www.pewclimate.org
/what_s_being_done/in_the_states/plug_-_in_electric_vehicles).

61. Lisa Schwartz, "Tour of Smart Grid Projects and State Policies,"
The Regulatory Assistance Project (Presentation to the Oregon Public Utility Commission, September 9, 2009).

62. "Utility-Scale Smart Meter Deployments, Plans & Proposals," Institute on Electric Efficiency, September 2011 (http://www .edisonfoundation.net/iee/issuebriefs/SmartMeter_Rollouts _0911.pdf).

63. Ibid.

64. See Edison Electric Institute for a summary of state actions in this area. Also, see the following for a summary of recent state level legislative and regulatory activities: "Demand Response & Smart Grid—State Legislative and Regulatory Policy Action Review: May 2010–June 2011," Association for Demand Response & Smart Grid.

65. Colorado Legislature Cuts Permit Fees for Solar Installations," Renewable Energy World Network, May 5, 2011 (http://www .renewableenergyworld.com/rea/news/article/2011/05/colorado -legislature-cuts-permit-fees-for-solar-installations).

66. See: "Solar Permitting Best Practices: Streamlining the Solar Permitting Process," The Vote Solar Initiative (http://votesolar.org/best-practices).

67. "Decision Adopting the Renewable Auction Mechanism," Rulemaking 08-08-009 before the Public Utilities Commission of the State of California, Filed August 21, 2009 (http://docs.cpuc.ca.gov/word_pdf /AGENDA_DECISION/127465.pdf).

68. "California approves reverse auction renewable energy market," Reuters, December 16, 2010 (http://blogs.reuters.com/environment /2010/12/16/california-approves-reverse-auction-renewable -energy-market).

69. "Connecticut HB 7432—*An Act Concerning Electricity and Energy Efficiency*: Sec. 21(1)," January 2007.

70. For a discussion of this issue, see: "The Effect of Private Wire Laws on Development of Combined Heat and Power Facilities: Pursuant to Section 1308 of EISA 2007," U.S. Department of Energy, January 12, 2009.

71. See: "Burrstone Energy Center LLC—Petition for a Declaratory Ruling That the Owner and Operator of a Proposed Cogeneration Facility Will Not Be Subject to Commission Jurisdiction: Declaratory Ruling on Exemption From Regulation," State of New York Public Service Commission Case 07-E-0802, August 22, 2007.

72. "California—Net Metering," Database of State Incentives for Renewables & Efficiency (DSIRE), Updated: October 13, 2011 (http://www.dsireusa .org/incentives/incentive.cfm?Incentive_Code=CA02R).

73. "Virtual Net Metering," California Public Utilities Commission, last modified: July 29, 2010 (http://www.cpuc.ca.gov/PUC/energy/DistGen /vnm.htm).

74. "Community Choice Aggregation," PG&E. (http://www.pge.com/cca).

75. "Community Choice Aggregation," Local Government Commission (http://www.lgc.org/cca/docs/cca_energy_factsheet.pdf).

76. "What is Community Choice Aggregation?" Local Government Commission (http://www.lgc.org/cca/what_is_cca.html).

77. "Community Choice Aggregation," Local Government Commission. (http://www.lgc.org/cca/docs/cca_energy_factsheet.pdf).

78. Molly F. Sherlock and Mark P. Keightley, "Master Limited Partnerships: A Policy Option for the Renewable Energy Industry," Congressional Research Service, June 28, 2011 (CRS 2011).

79. Ibid.

80. Ibid.

81. John Joshi and Malay Bansal, "The Case For Master Limited Partnerships," AOL Energy, July 20, 2011.

Chapter 5

1. The survey instrument was also used to supplement the outreach to other selected stakeholders, including utilities.

2. This was a comment from a utility that was passed along by one of the participants in our outreach.

3. One former PUC chairman also noted an indirectly-related issue for state utility regulatory commissions: "Another problem with state regulation is the relatively short life of a commissioner's term— average service life is 2.7 years. We need to account for lack of experience. There is also more partisanship in state regulation than there used to be."

4. This is not a new observation: nearly a decade ago, one major assessment on distributed energy resources noted that "for distributed generation to be successful, the utility business and regulatory model need to be

changed." See: Amory B. Lovins et al, *Small is Profitable: The Hidden Economic Benefits of Making Electrical Resources the Right Size* (Colorado: Rocky Mountain Institute, 2002), 356.

5. FERC already plays a role, and both EE and DR are actively bid into the wholesale markets in ISO New England and PJM today.

6. This issue is not related solely to DPS (many other resources could benefit from PRD as well), and is under discussion by multiple policymakers, regulators, and other stakeholders.

7. It should be noted that net metering and interconnection standards are being changed and updated at the state level on an ongoing basis. The Network for New Energy Choices documents these revisions in state-level policies each year and grades them in its annual report. See: "Freeing the Grid: Best Practices in State Net Metering Policies and Interconnection Procedures," Network for New Energy Choices, December 2010. Also note that "IEEE 1547.4—Guide for Design, Operation, and Integration of Distributed Resource Island Systems with Electric Power Systems" was published in July 2011. See the IEEE Standards Association website at http://grouper.ieee.org/groups /scc21/1547.4/1547.4_index.html.

8. According to one participant in our outreach, some utilities require the DG system owner to pay $1 million of upgrades for each MW of capacity.

9. Anna Chittum and Nate Kaufman, "Challenges Facing Combined Heat and Power Today: A State-by-State Assessment," ACEEE Report No. IE111, p.iii, forthcoming.

10. There are also some incentives below the state level: one participant noted that the only FIT for CHP in the country is in place in the Sacramento Municipal Utility District.

11. Another participant noted, however, that frequency regulation in PJM is 1 percent of a day's peak, so for storage this is a small market.

Chapter 6

1. Several of these recommendations build on those outlined by the California Energy Commission in "Distributed Generation Strategic Plan," California Energy Commission, June 2002, 21 (http://www .energy.ca.gov/reports/2002-06-12_700-02-002.PDF).

2. A much more basic and potentially intractable challenge is that a foundational policy (or set of policies) assumes strong consensus on objectives and, unfortunately, that does not seem to exist currently, especially with regard to climate change and the need to move to a de-carbonized economy. This discussion is clearly beyond the scope of this paper; however, we start from the assumption that meeting the challenge of climate change is central to energy policy development.

3. For more detail on this proposal see Ren Orans et al, "A Modest Proposal: After Cap and Trade," Brookings Press, June 2010.

4. "A Business Plan for America's Energy Future," American Energy Innovation Council, September 2011 (AEIC 2011).

5. Ibid, p. 16.

6. "ARPA-E Mission Statement," http://arpa-e.energy.gov/About/Mission .aspx. ARPA-E is supporting DPS—it held a workshop in June 2011 on small-scale distributed generation in which "the meeting's output will help direct the actions of ARPA-E towards the most promising and appropriate high risk, high return R&D funding opportunities and management strategies."

7. AEIC 2011, p. 26.

8. "Energy Transformation Acceleration Fund, Advanced Research Projects Agency—Energy: Proposed Appropriation Language," ARPA-E. http://arpa-e.energy.gov/LinkClick.aspx?fileticket =otZens1luj0%3d&tabid=184.

9. AEIC 2011, 5.

10. "Overview and Status of Update of §1603 Program, U.S. Department of Treasury, September 11, 2011. http://www.treasury.gov/initiatives /recovery/Documents/2011-09-11%20-%20S1603%20Overview%20 -%20No%20Maps.pdf.

11. Bipartisan Policy Center 2011, 13.

12. Ibid, pp. 16–19.

13. "Industrial Distributed Energy: Clean Energy Application Centers," U.S. DOE Energy Efficiency & Renewable Energy (http://www1.eere .energy.gov/industry/distributedenergy/racs.html).

14. Tom Key and Matt Wakefield, "Smart Grid Demonstrations: Focus on Integrating Distributed Energy Resources," *EPRI Journal* (Winter 2010),

pp. 21–23 (http://mydocs.epri.com/docs/CorporateDocuments /EPRI_Journal/2010-Winter/1022333_SmartGridDemo.pdf).

15. See Grants and Research: American Recovery and Reinvestment Act, National Association of Regulatory Utility Commissioners. Accessed at (http://www.naruc.org/grants/programs.cfm?page=63).

16. Dan Rastler, "Small Scale Distributed Generation: Perspectives on Markets and Challenges and Opportunities," Electric Power Research Institute (presentation at ARPA-E Workshop, 1–2, June 2011) (http:// arpa-e.energy.gov/LinkClick.aspx?fileticket=3PKUCIyA3Ww%3D& tabid=437).

17. Solyndra's bankruptcy was due to a number of factors—including falling silicon prices (which impacted the competitiveness of Solyndra's non-silicon-based technology) and alleged impropriety of loan oversight—which are beyond the scope of this paper.

18. Mark Muro and Jonathan Rothwell, "Why the U.S. Should Not Abandon Its Clean Energy Lending Programs," The Brookings Institution, October 9, 2011. http://www.up-front/posts/2011/09/27 -solyndra=muro=rothwell.

19. Supporters argue that for every dollar of federal spending, the loan guarantee program yields $4–8 of private lending. The Office of Management and Budget has estimated that the government's loan guarantees across all sectors of the economy will return $46 billion to taxpayers in 2011 (see Muro and Rothwell, September 2011). Opponents believe that while government support for clean technology development through sustained R&D is vital, the inherent conflicts of interest that arise in loan-guarantee programs make them an inappropriate choice for government policy. In addition, these observers point out that, at the time of writing, there is the possibility that taxpayers will recoup little or nothing of their investment in Solyndra in which taxpayers had their debt subordinated to private investors.

20. "President Obama signs an Executive Order Focused on Federal Leadership in Environmental, Energy, and Economic Performance," The White House Office of the Press Secretary, October 5, 2009.

21. This builds on Executive Order 13423, "Strengthening Federal Environmental, Energy, and Transportation Management," signed on January 24, 2007.

22. See Executive Order 13514, "Federal Leadership in Environmental, Energy, and Economic Performance," Sections 2(a)ii, and 2(f)ii.

23. "Department of Defense Base Structure Report, Fiscal Year 2007 Deadline." (http://www.defense.gov/pubs/BSR_2007_Baseline .pdfhttp://www.defense.gov/pubs/BSR_2007_Baseline.pdf).

24. "State Electric Efficiency Regulatory Frameworks," Institute for Electric Efficiency, June 2011.

25. For example, see: "Community Renewables: Model Program Rules," Interstate Renewable Energy Council, November 2010.

26. See: "Public Utilities Commission of the State of California Resolution E-4414," CPUC, 18 August 2011 (http://docs.cpuc.ca.gov/WORD_PDF /FINAL_RESOLUTION/141795.PDF).

27. "Next Generation Energy Act of 2007," HF436/SF145*/CH136, Public Information Services, Minnesota House of Representatives (http:// www.house.leg.state.mn.us/hinfo/newlawsart2007-0.asp?yearid=2007 &storyid=608).

28. "Chapter 4901:1–39," Public Utilities Commission of Ohio—Energy, Jobs, Progress: Ohio Senate Bill 221 (http://www.puco.ohio.gov/puco /index.cfm/consumer-information/consumer-topics/energy-jobs -progress-ohio-senate-bill-221).

29. "California Incentives/Policies for Renewables & Efficiency: Energy Efficiency Resource Standard," Database of State Incentives for Renewables & Efficiency (DSIRE), last reviewed: 6 January 2011 (http:// www.dsireusa.org/incentives/incentive.cfm?Incentive_Code =CA62R&re=1&ee=1).

30. "Storage Technology of Renewable and Green Energy Act of 2009 (STORAGE)," United States Senator Ron Wyden—Issues and Legisla- tion (http://wyden.senate.gov/issues/legislation/details/?id=ca1be51d -95e0-4128-ad44-4bc53828c36f&p=ac76c3bb-af2f-4049-9c10 -ca77fbd00e6b).

31. For example, Oak Ridge National Laboratory compiled a report in May 2011 on policy options to promote energy efficiency. The report echoed the CHP industry's call for output-based emissions standards, tax incentives, and a federal energy portfolio standard with CHP, as well as other measures including property-assessed clean energy financing and energy efficiency rebates. Marilyn A. Brown et al, "Making Industry

Part of the Climate Solution: Policy Options to Promote Efficiency," Oak Ridge National Laboratory, May 2011.
32. Energy Security in Critical Government Infrastructure, GP Feasibility Studies for Critical Government Buildings and Facilities (http://www.txsecurepower.org).

Annex 2

1. Defined by FERC as "the potential for lost revenue on the part of utilities and practices such as standby charges, retail natural gas rates for wholesale applications, exit fees, and sell-back rates."

ABOUT THE AUTHORS

John Banks is a nonresident fellow at the Energy Security Initiative at Brookings. He specializes in working with governments, companies, and regulators in establishing and strengthening policies, institutions, and regulatory frameworks that promote sustainable energy sectors, with a focus on emerging markets and electricity. Banks has worked in more than twenty countries. He is also an adjunct professor for electricity markets at the Johns Hopkins School of Advanced International Studies and for energy policy at the Georgetown University School of Foreign Service.

Jeremy Carl is a research fellow at the Hoover Institution and a member of the Shultz-Stephenson Task Force on Energy Policy. His work focuses on energy and environmental policy, with an emphasis on energy security and global fossil fuel markets. Before coming to Hoover, Carl was a research fellow at the Program on Energy and Sustainable Development at Stanford and a visiting fellow in resource and development economics at the Energy and Resources Institute in New Delhi, India. His writing and expertise have been featured in the *New York Times*, *Wall Street Journal*, *Newsweek*, and many other publications. He holds degrees in history and public policy from Yale and Harvard Universities.

David Fedor is a research analyst on the Hoover Institution's Shultz-Stephenson Task Force on Energy Policy. He has worked in energy and the environment across China, Japan, and the United States. Formerly at APEC's Asia Pacific Energy Research Center and Stanford's Collaboratory for Research on Global Projects, Fedor has also consulted for WWF China, the Asian Development Bank, and the Korea Energy Economics Institute. He holds degrees in earth systems from Stanford University.

Kevin Massy is assistant director of the Energy Security Initiative at Brookings, where he manages research into international energy relations and domestic energy policy. A former journalist, most recently for *The Economist* magazine, he has written widely on the role of emerging technologies in the energy sector. Massy holds degrees in international business and journalism from Georgetown University, City University London, and the University of Newcastle.

Pedram Mokrian is a venture capitalist focused on the energy-tech sector at Mayfield Fund. Before Mayfield he was on the commodities trading desk at Credit Suisse and held positions at Ford Motor Company, JDS Uniphase, and Nortel Networks. In addition to his contributions to the Shultz-Stephenson Task Force on Energy Policy, he serves on the board of the San Francisco Bay Area Chapter of the Young Professionals in Energy and is a charter member of C100. Mokrian holds degrees from Stanford University including a PhD in energy finance and economics.

Jelena Simjanović is emerging markets lead at Thomson Reuters Point Carbon and a former senior research assistant on the Hoover Institution's Shultz-Stephenson Task Force on Energy Policy. She specializes in energy and carbon markets and clean technology finance. Simjanović has consulted on energy and climate issues in the United States, Europe, and Asia with the World Bank, Alliance to Save Energy, and the California Attorney General's Office. Fluent in four languages, she holds degrees in energy and resources and in public policy from the University of California at Berkeley.

David Slayton came to Hoover as a U.S. Navy national security affairs fellow after his command tour with the Electronic Attack Squadron 134. During his career, he has deployed twelve times and participated in a broad range of combat operations on the ground, at sea, and in the air, conducting numerous combat missions into Afghanistan and Iraq. A career naval flight officer, he has flown more than three hundred combat missions. His research focuses on the electromagnetic spectrum, maritime strategy, and future energy sources, transmission, and infrastructure. Slayton holds degrees from the University of California at Los Angeles, the University of San Diego, and the Naval War College.

Amy Guy Wagner is senior consultant at Energy and Environmental Economics, E3, where she leads project work in its emerging technology practice with clients including BrightSource

Energy, SunEdison, Electric Power Research Institute, and the California Public Utilities Commission. Her work includes utility valuation, strategic siting, transmission risk assessment, and investor support. Wagner also assisted Hawaiian Electric Company in its feed-in tariff proceeding, developing rates for small-scale wind, photovoltaics, concentrating solar power, and in-line hydro projects. She holds degrees in earth systems and energy policy and strategy from Stanford University.

Lisa Wood is the executive director of IEE, an institute of the Edison Foundation focused on Innovation, Electricity, and Efficiency and nonresident fellow at the Energy Security Initiative at Brookings Institution. Wood launched IEE after more than two decades consulting with electric utilities on retail customer issues. Through numerous articles, dialogues, and speaking engagements, she contributes to the conversation on innovation in the power sector, smart technology, smart pricing, energy efficiency, distributed power, and customer-side issues. Wood is also an adjunct professor at the Georgetown University School of Foreign Service.

About the Hoover Institution's
SHULTZ-STEPHENSON TASK FORCE
ON ENERGY POLICY

The Hoover Institution's Shultz-Stephenson Task Force on Energy Policy addresses energy policy in the United States and its effects on our domestic and international political priorities, particularly our national security.

As a result of volatile and rising energy prices and increasing global concern about climate change, two related and compelling issues—threats to national security and adverse effects of energy usage on global climate—have emerged as key adjuncts to America's energy policy; the task force will explore these subjects in detail. The task force's goals are to gather comprehensive information on current scientific and technological developments, survey the contingent policy actions, and offer a range of prescriptive policies to address our varied energy challenges. The task force will focus on public policy at all levels, from individual to global. It will then recommend policy initiatives, large and small, that can be undertaken to the advantage of both private enterprises and governments acting individually and in concert.

Contact for the Shultz-Stephenson
Task Force on Energy Policy:
Jeremy Carl, *Research Fellow*
(650) 723-2136
carljc@stanford.edu

About the

ꓐ | Energy Security Initiative
at BROOKINGS

The Energy Security Initiative (ESI) is a cross-program effort by the Brookings Institution designed to foster multidisciplinary research and dialogue on all aspects of energy security. ESI recognizes that public and private choices related to energy production and use will shape the global economic, environmental and strategic landscape in profound ways and that achieving a more secure future will therefore require a determined effort to understand the likely consequences of these choices and their implications for sound policymaking. The ESI Policy Brief Series is intended to showcase serious and focused scholarship on topical issues in one or more of these broad research areas, with an emphasis on targeted policy recommendations.

Brookings recognizes that the value it provides to any supporter is in its absolute commitment to quality, independence and impact. Activities supported by its donors reflect this commitment, and the analysis and recommendations of the Institution's scholars are not determined by any donation.

Contact for the Energy Security Initiative:
Govinda Avasarala, *Research Assistant*
(202) 797-6231
gavasarala@brookings.edu

INDEX

HOOVER INSTITUTION

SHULTZ-STEPHENSON TASK FORCE ON
Energy Policy

*Books published by members
and contributors of the*
SHULTZ-STEPHENSON TASK FORCE
ON ENERGY POLICY

Distributed Power in the United States:
Prospects and Policies
Edited by Jeremy Carl
HOOVER INSTITUTION PRESS, 2013

Powering the Armed Forces:
Meeting the Military's Energy Challenges
Gary Roughead, Jeremy Carl, and Manuel Hernandez
HOOVER INSTITUTION PRESS, 2012

Corn Ethanol: Who Pays? Who Benefits?
Ken G. Glozer
HOOVER INSTITUTION PRESS, 2011

Beyond Smoke and Mirrors:
Climate Change and Energy in the 21st Century
Burton Richter
CAMBRIDGE UNIVERSITY PRESS, 2011

Conversations about Energy:
How the Experts See America's Energy Choices
Edited by Jeremy Carl and James Goodby
HOOVER INSTITUTION PRESS, 2010